Reach for a Star and Generate Ideas for Innovation

Tools for Creating Your Innovation Project for Business or School

Reach for a Star and Generate Ideas for Innovation

Tools for Creating Your Innovation Project for Business or School

CARLOS S. MONSIVÁIS

Applegate Valley
Publishing

Reach for a Star and Generate Ideas for Innovation:
Tools for Creating Your Innovation Project for Business or School
Carlos S. Monsiváis

Copyright ©2021 Carlos S. Monsiváis
First English Edition: May 2021

ISBN: 978-1-7370685-1-8
Copyright © 2021
Library of Congress Control Number: 2021908272

Original title of the book in Spanish:
Baja una Estrella y Generarás Ideas = Innovación
Herramientas para elaborar tu proyecto de innovación en negocio o escuela

English translation by Michael Brunelle and B. Cortabarria

© Layout and cover design: Illumination Graphics
© Picture of astronaut: DepositPhotos.com

Applegate Valley Publishing
All inquiries should be addressed to:
info@applegatevalleypublishing.com
Grants Pass, OR 97527

Printed in USA

For my children, Carlos Servando and Mildred E.,
for their friendship and character.

I would also like to thank the Great Chief for his
teachings and universal wisdom.

Contents

About the Author

Carlos S. Monsiváis is a fisheries biologist by profession, a graduate of the Universidad Autónoma de Sinaloa, Mexico. He studied project management at the University of Alaska Anchorage. He enjoys writing about the subjects of innovation and idea generation. Carlos has worked in the United States, Japan, Mexico, New Zealand, and Taiwan. In addition, he has received awards for innovation from the Technology, Research, and Development Center (TREND), United States, in 2006, 2007, 2008, and 2012. He has also participated as a principal researcher in innovation projects in aquaculture and fisheries and competitive projects for economic subsidies from the United States Department of Agriculture Small Business Innovation Research (USDA SBIR) program.

During his career, he has written about subjects related to tuna-dolphin behavior and association in the eastern Pacific Ocean. He has also been a researcher in the biology and population dynamics of salmon in rivers in the state of Alaska. In addition, he has worked in the government and industrial fishing sectors on cod, herring, halibut, salmon, crab, octopus, squid, shrimp, tuna, and billfish.

Carlos has spent the past four years writing innovative projects in the field of fisheries. He will use the proceeds from this book to initiate the research and development of a biomedical project. He has two children and resides in California.

Reach for a Star and Generate Ideas for Innovation:
Tools for Creating Your Innovation Project for Business or School

To explain the title, this book uses the star to represent the timeline of our lives; like us, stars are born, they develop, and they die. In a process that is similar to this, you can generate an idea for innovation, a new and change-making project, and that is the purpose of this book.

The drawing on the cover is an eight-pointed blue star, which is the number of chapters in this book. The color yellow represents the day star, the sun, and the two stars sit on a universal violet ring inside a green circle, which represents the completion of your project.

This is the first of a series of texts that are intended to simplify and recreate ideas and concepts, and to transform them into innovative projects. This book is designed for university students, technicians, and anybody who is interested in working on innovative projects.

Preface

Thank you for buying this book. I wish you an excellent journey with **Reach for a Star and Generate Ideas for Innovation:** *Tools for Creating Your Innovation Project for Business or School.*

On our planet, the creative innovation projects were originally undertaken by the indigenous civilizations who inhabited these lands, primarily for the purpose of ensuring their survival. These native cultures still exist today. Their innovations began with the construction of their houses, their agriculture, the development of crafts, ways of conserving food, natural medicine, temples, natural resources, astronomy, and even the invention of calendars for the projection and organization of their daily and future activities.

Nowadays, the number of scientific innovations generated is minimal and will continue to be so for years. For this reason, success is up to you, as a young enthusiast and initiator of projects. Reproducing ideas, playing, and recombining knowledge, will help you fully develop a plan by using your experience, intelligence, and creativity to develop great new ideas.

You must initiate this idea with careful observation to imagine it and sort it out in your mind, record it in a final document, and finally bring it to conclusion with a project.

Actually, this book contains a variety of tools that will allow you to diversify any concept or idea that you generate.

Here you will find the methods and means of innovation needed to develop and finalize any project in a variety of fields, whether they are for work or for innovation projects in school. You might be familiar with, or have tried to follow, various books about developing business plans or innovation projects, and they can be interesting. In this book, you will learn these concepts.

☆ **Use your imagination to visualize.** That is, closely observe what you see and what might not be real or actual. This ability to see beyond using your imagination is alluded to by the scientist Albert Einstein in his famous quote, "Imagination is more important than knowledge."

☆ **Create a storm of specific and persistent ideas.** These ideas will be based on breaking down information that your mind will process at a highly developed level, and this book will help you to do the following.

1. Elaborate your plan for innovation based on the initial idea that you come up with.

2. Strengthen the idea in a consistent manner, that is, extract and use all the nutrients from the concept and diversify it.

3. Use your creativity as a base and catalyst to increase its usefulness and fully develop any idea you have and carry it to fruition.

☆ **Think in a simple basic manner.** Remember our past civilizations and their **tradition-innovation-continuity.**

☆ **Transform a project into a process.** This means providing guidance from the moment you have a strong vision of an idea to the development of models for professional and technical-scientific projects, where you develop concepts and then shape them into innovation plans for various industries, such as cosmetics, hand tools and gardening, transportation, government, solar energy, and packaging, among others, as well as for professional fields, such as applied engineering, medicine, biotechnology, artificial intelligence, among others, or just an innovation project for your school assignment.

You can follow and complete this circle of eight chapters in a simple, clear, and easy to understand manner.

The most important reason for tackling an innovation project is to activate three innate skills, which are represented in the following illustration.

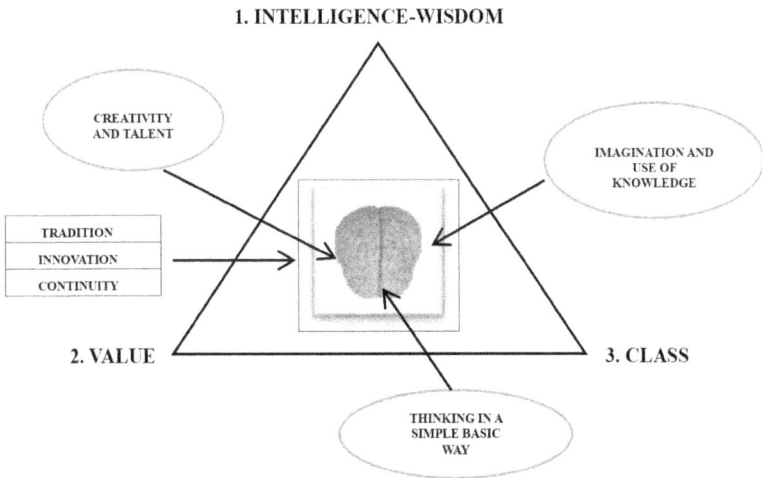

1. INTELLIGENCE-WISDOM

CREATIVITY AND TALENT

IMAGINATION AND USE OF KNOWLEDGE

TRADITION
INNOVATION
CONTINUITY

2. VALUE

3. CLASS

THINKING IN A SIMPLE BASIC WAY

☆ Intelligence-Wisdom

This is the full knowledge of what is certain, what is correct, and what is lasting in your idea that can be transformed into a business plan or homework assignment. You will do this by creatively using your exceptional imagination and balancing knowledge and development. This way you will end up with a final document that you will be able to submit for any type of venture capital or economic funding to initiate your successful innovation.

☆ Value

The confidence of having a well-defined idea enables you to make decisions and helps you understand the great value of the idea or project that you are creating. It strongly influences the development of your proposal in a decisive and steadfast way. Remember, tradition-innovation-continuity, the key to creating change.

☆ Class

You will see this concept in the quality of, and ability to comprehend, the change that you are creating, whether individually or collectively. Think simply and stay with the basics. You will have specific goals and objectives that will lead you to a conclusion, strategies that will give you direction, and class upon arriving at your innovative results.

Acknowledgments

In the first place, I must extend my deep gratitude to all of the people who in one way or another supported me in accomplishing this project. To all of my teachers for their contribution to the knowledge I have acquired during this long journey, in which the combination of theory, practice, and experience have enabled me to use those skills to achieve and further the development of any innovation project.

Thank you to my brother Fernando Gilberto for teaching me how to describe the planning and development of design projects in a single page with illustrations of how you can play with ideas, use creativity, and how to develop great projects.

Finally, I would like to recognize the help and complete support of the seven family gems during the writing of this book.

Introduction

The central idea of ***Reach for a Star and Generate Ideas for Innovation:*** *Tools for Creating Your Innovation Project for Work or School* is that in many fields and production sectors there should always be a new initiative, creativity with imaginative ability, as well as enthusiasm for the natural existence of new projects, fair competition, and the creation of new models. This way you will be able to complete a project that will include a final document that will help you put together a new business or to simply create an innovation project for a school assignment.

We can divide these projects into two types.

☆ New projects or innovations that are completely original.

☆ Reinvented projects for an existing business using the innovation process.

On the following pages, I will lay out the process for the creative development of new or innovative projects in a format that includes eight sections with the individual summaries of the chapters that follow, where the appropriate terminology for the development of a dynamic project is introduced. In addition, there are descriptions of the basic strategic principles that should be followed and applied in combination, in the case of an existing business, to achieve excellence and success in the product, service, or result that you wish to develop. You can apply them to establish a new or existing business, generate new ideas and thus increase its productivity. In this manner, you will create healthy competition within a global market, where all aspects of the innovative process become more demanding every day.

This book begins with Section 1, called Your Idea, and Chapter 1, titled Visualizing the Potential of an Idea, and concludes with Section 8, titled End of the Circle of Innovation, and with Chapter 8, called Finalizing the Innovation Project.

In the book, the sections and the chapters offer an overall description that provides all the tools needed for completing an innovation project. With these, you will be able to develop projects and innovate in different areas, thanks to the helpful model diagrams that will guide you to the end of the project and writing of a final document, which will help you compete for grants. These grants are available in different areas of your field, which will help you establish a business, a new product, a service, or complete an innovative school project.

In each chapter, there is an explanation that begins with generating an idea and ends with carrying it to a conclusion, in other words, following a process that culminates in your desired product, service, or result with easy-to-follow diagrams and figures that act as guides and explanations. You will be able to manage your own project in a simple and practical manner.

With this book, you can address the fundamental issues in the process of configuring an idea, administering all the details related to a project, and finding financial backing to begin innovating. This way you will combine your creativity with the exposure needed to succeed in any kind of innovation and field. You will create a project plan to transform that original thought into any type of innovation, where you can explore a service, product, or subproduct of any element that you can imagine. You will understand, know, and strategically develop everything related to the knowledge that you acquire. In doing so, you will break down any barriers that arise and come to understand the scope of the innovation, creating opportunities for moving forward, always looking further ahead, from within the project. I recommend following the titles of the eight sections and chapters that are briefly explained here sequentially.

In Chapter 1, I analyze the framework for visualizing the potential of an idea. You will make observations using any image that represents the creation of a concept. This will help you generate a storm of ideas that you can use to form a descriptive image of the possibilities, and then lay out a clear structure to carry it to completion as an innovation project. Then you will use the structure as a guide for the development of the project. Illustrating this image will create a mental model by giving it a more visual and concrete form. With the use and perspective of this powerful idea-image that you created, your imagination will wander into the past, the present, and toward the future. This way you will be able to turn to a specific concept for the development of a product, service, or result, and develop it into an innovation that might be the start of a business or a school project.

Chapter 2 explores how to structure an idea. In doing so, you will represent your initial concept using a diagram in which you will insert brief comments as feedback to the idea. This will help you explore in greater depth concepts related to organization, development, use, and technology, among others. This way you will discover and make use of any opportunities that result from the idea. In this configuration, you will express the different forms, with general and specific options, that are available with the tools that are given to you and which you will use for the full benefit of the great idea without losing your main focus. That means squeezing everything from the idea itself, to help you discover all aspects of the concept during the product development process.

This is how you can think about the product, service, or specific result that you generate while innovating.

Chapter 3 examines the main resources for implementing the process of developing an innovation. While working on your idea for any concept that you want to promote, you can emphasize research and the creation of a prototype of the final project as a technical-scientific document, which is needed for carrying out your innovation and applying it to a specific field. You will come to understand the methodology that is used and described in each section that contains this type of model diagram that represents the kind of innovation that you can carry out to start a business, make a new discovery, or for a school project.

Chapter 4 covers the initiation of the innovation project. It consists of outlining the first activities of the group involved in the management of a project, the life cycle of an innovation project, and a model and diagram of the phases of a project in the area of a given profession. Also outlined are the successes of a project and general aspects during the initiation of an idea and the transition to a new phase of your innovation concept.

Chapter 5 shows a complete strategy for the planning of a project. I point out the importance of making a good plan for everything you do, while working on a proposal for an innovation. You will design an outline or a simple sectioned guide for optimal organization and coordination. Good planning is an art, therefore you want to always use it when laying out the activities that are to be carried out in the future.

Chapter 6 presents information about project management. You will use five key elements to help you manage all of the objectives, activities, and responsibilities in running an innovation project. Additionally, while working on a creative concept, you will introduce the strategies, resources, time, and budget that you will use in the process of developing a project. You should begin by establishing an order and using all available tools in its development, whether for an organization or for a project for a variety of purposes in a variety of entrepreneurial areas.

The monitoring and control of the execution of a project is laid out in Chapter 7. This is where you will continuously verify and examine the progress of the objectives, budget, scope, and the limits of the innovations that you are beginning to implement. You will also describe all the components that support, collectively and efficiently, the application of the system, monitoring all changes that will occur during the implementation of the activities laid out in the plan. You will describe all the components that collectively and efficiently support the monitoring system and exert an effective control during the innovation process.

Finally, in Chapter 8, I describe the basic elements of the completion of the project. Here I will show how to carry your project to fruition or the conclusion of the innovation cycle.

You will end up with a well-thought-out and illustrated idea containing the specific points that you must use to verify the progress toward the completion of a project with the following elements: the conclusion of operations of your experimental design, the scope of management functions, and the presentation of your vision to everyone who participates in the completion of the circle of innovation.

I hope that in the following pages you will find insightful concepts and advice that you can apply to your advantage in leveraging the ideas, first steps, development, management, and execution of innovation projects, together with the backing of a variety of available grants. Finally, the purpose and most important goal is for you to end up with a new discovery, a splendid business, and successful school project. Forward! This will be the best reward for your work.

SECTION 1

YOUR IDEA

The process and technique for visualizing an idea is a continuous exercise, and ideas exist all around us in this diverse world. Innovation is born from an imaginative vision that when put to work can be processed, documented, developed, and used to generate data to create a product, service, or result that you wish to pursue. Visualization is a powerful tool that can help you generate a concept with a perspective that you can turn into innovation.

In the time between generating ideas and their development, there is a technique for representing them that will help you break down the different components so you can experiment with them and analyze them, with the goal of collecting preliminary data for your idea or final concept.

CHAPTER 1

VISUALIZING THE POTENTIAL OF AN IDEA

How do you spot an idea? How do you innovate with that idea? What model can you use to trigger that idea and turn it into an innovation project? What impact will the transformation and innovation of that idea have? What strategies will you use for growing and developing that grand idea?

These are some of the questions that you will ask yourself as you progress and work toward the realization of your idea, using the tools that are presented in this book for developing it, assuming that you find no roadblocks in your journey that will prevent you from launching your innovation project. Whether you are establishing your own business or simply working on a school assignment about innovation, you should form and process certain ideas that excite you and that you would enjoy doing as a project. This way you will begin to develop an innovative plan. Then you will be able to use the ideas, processes, and tools that I offer in this book, which are essential and will be useful for the development and advancement of a project.

In this chapter, you are going to answer some questions from the Imagery Representation Model, which are shown with examples, and that can be answered to help develop the idea that you generate. Next, you will be able to use the following chapters to project, produce, and structure the great idea with the goal of developing a project, which together with all the components will be become part of the implementation of the plan. However, it will be easy to use and will give you a better grasp of your vision, which will be turned into an interesting and creative result.

The visualization of an idea is a powerful technique, in which you create an image of the desired result, making it as detailed as possible. It is a matter of feeling and experiencing the final result. In this way you will carry the innovation process of your grand idea to fruition. I wish you great success and enjoy the journey. Let's get started.

How to Start Innovating?

Our indigenous cultures began innovating as a necessity in a productive, imaginative, and simple way to satisfy their needs relying on an array of innate tools that they had in their minds. Then, they further developed it to come up with results that solved their problems and generated new discoveries that revolved around their survival, the main common denominator.

The word *innovation* comes from the Latin *innovatio*. This concept is used in the sense of creating new ideas and making discoveries, as illustrated in Figure 1.1, showing the process of transformation that guides you in conceptualizing a new product, service, or result and then designing and documenting the innovation.

Figure 1.1

Representation of an Innovation

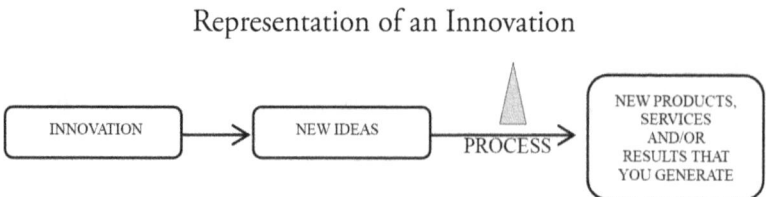

| INNOVATION | → | NEW IDEAS | PROCESS → | NEW PRODUCTS, SERVICES AND/OR RESULTS THAT YOU GENERATE |

Our resolute innovative ancestors had an intelligence and ability that sometimes confounds the imagination. The people of indigenous cultures were true pioneers. It is important to point out that these civilizations helped humankind advance, which is why they occupy an important place in the history of innovation.

What Kind of Tools Did They Use?

These cultures did not have instructions for solving their problems. They used their imagination to the fullest, as seen in the way they maximized the use, viability, and development of their resources. It is important to be prepared to use the idea that you generate and to maximize every aspect of its functionality and usefulness.

Remember that the imagination is like the open sky, where a bird glides and soars. I want you to immerse yourself in this exercise and its transformative power. The ancient cultures applied imaginative solutions to their difficult problems and showed an ability to combine materials and components in new ways, therefore generating new solutions. Their intelligence demonstrated determination, thinking differently and in a way that was not limited by the idea of "that is the way that it has always been done." A creative mind is uninhibited and free. "Whatever the mind of man can conceive and believe, it can achieve" (Napoleon Hill, American author).

In the process, you will take your concept on a journey, and you will carry it to fruition with a storm of ideas. Include the questions you will ask, the models and the feedback for the idea you launched, and I am sure that you will be surprised by the number of creative and innovative options that you come up with. All great journeys begin with a big idea and initiative, imagination, planning, direction, and expression; this is the way I want you to get started and proceed to turn your idea into a great innovation.

We will break down the entire structure of the thinking process for the development of your original idea in a concise and straightforward format to make visualization easier. When it comes to innovation, you should approach your vision with an open mind, a clear and flexible attitude, and nimble thinking. Capture your concept in a way that will successfully generate results when using this transformative process.

What Prevents You from Seeing the Idea?

In the room where I am writing this book, there is a painting, shown in Figure 1.2. It is an example of how to generate ideas. You begin the transformation process toward ideation by fully engaging in the search for a concept that will creatively use all the content that you observe in the picture.

Figure 1.2

An Example of How to Generate Ideas

Carefully observe the details of this painting. Look at it from a specific vantage point and make a mental note of every component that you notice in the representation. This process is called "photographic observation."

You should analyze it carefully and think about how you can transform all the details that you observe, the symbols, the figures, signs, and everything you see to generate an idea and transform it into an innovation; do this thoroughly. In this example, you can see the following.

1. Plants/leaves.
2. Flowers (petals).
3. Wood frame.

4. Material it is painted on.
5. Stand where the flowers are placed.
6. Paint.

These elements will help you gain a perspective or understanding of all the components of an image to help you generate innovative ideas and create other applications and uses for them. In this example, you could think about using the plants and flowers for medicinal purposes or for the field of telemedicine.

You will utilize the necessary tools described in this book to find one or several opportunities to use each material that you identify. Based on the observations that you make, ask yourself what product, service, or result you can generate. You can come up with a new idea using these materials that you observe and transform them into one or more of these ideas.

• New product, subproduct, or service.
• New process.
• New business model.
• New use for an existing product.
• New market for existing products.
• New distribution channels.
• Discovery of a subproduct during the innovation process.

The representation or visualized image will immediately transport you to archetypal forms, like the ones that were used by our indigenous cultures, who were the first innovators on the planet. Then you will visualize modern applications for your product or service and finally transform it into a tool or service that together with other existing practices or concepts can become a successful and cutting-edge business. You can make connections or correlations with your vision or simply search for promising combinations among old and new ideas to give the innovation a creative use.

To help you with visualization, you should use the Imagery Representation Model. This version of the model can be applied to generate a storm of ideas in any field. The link between the ideas that you come up with and developing them involves researching and exploring keywords for basic processes that you will be using. You will break down the idea with logical questions related to the concept that you generate and be able to create a preliminary draft before you commit your project into writing. You should be able to access information and statistics for your country, financial data, and census records on the internet, and analyze everything pertaining to your idea as it relates to the product or service, which might be helpful for the implementation of your business concept.

The Imagery Representation Model can be summed up in six keywords, which are represented in Figure 1.3, that you can always use as a quick reference for any idea that you generate. By using the six keywords in the model, you will obtain the most relevant and insightful data. Later you will see an illustration of the model in use.

Figure 1.3

Keywords of the Imagery Representation Model

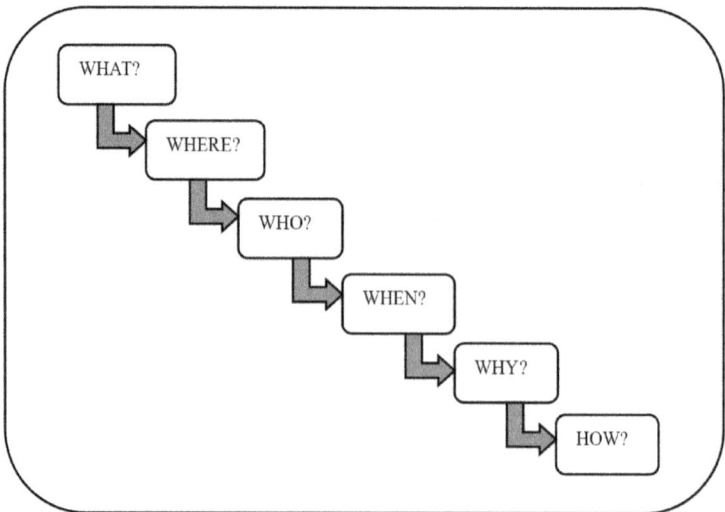

Next, take a look at each of these six keywords in the model, which is an example of the practical and functional way in which you can handle the storm of ideas to analyze them. There are many possible questions, and you can add more based on the ideas that you are exploring. Generally, you will use these six words from the model to analyze your idea.

The first factor or element of the Imagery Representation Model is **what.** As represented in Figure 1.4, **what** is your idea? You can follow this model based on the type of innovation that you are working on. By following the process represented here, you should be able to analyze and obtain results, which will help you begin to make the transformation into a product, subproduct, or service. By doing this you will create and refine your ideogram, which will result in an image or photographic observation that you will use to pursue your great idea.

This will be your most important step. Starting here, you will detail every representation, symbol, figure, or image that you can think of to develop them into an innovation. You should consider every angle of the creation that you come up with, which will help you develop a new product, new process, new business model, new uses for existing products, new markets for existing products, new distribution channels, and discover new products, subproducts, or services. All this will contribute to transforming and innovating in a unique and creative manner. You will be able to combine images and turn them into a central idea.

Using the same method, you will be able to describe all of the uses to create an image. You will describe the entire service in the same way, which will produce a representation or image for you. Typically, a product, service, or result that you are working on can generate multiple uses in different industries, as long as it is developed with a goal in mind, which would be effecting a change or creating a system that results in the innovation of a product, which gets the attention of the consumer.

Remember, consumers are going to be your ultimate quality control at the end of the long process of conceptualization, creation, and testing. Ultimately, they will be the judges of everything you develop and make. This is why throughout the entire exercise you are processing the idea using your best judgment, professionalism, and clear vision in the course of taking this idea to fruition to achieve a top-quality product. You should be thinking about your product as being unique and the best in terms of its methodology and elaboration and still be competitive and attractive to a demanding consumer, should the final result be different from the original idea.

Figure 1.4

Imagery Representation Model

TABLE 1

WHAT PRODUCT, SUB-PRODUCT, SERVICE AND/OR RESULT THAT YOU ARE UNDERTAKING WILL GENERATE THIS IMAGE?

STAR SOLVER

WHAT IS YOUR IDEA?

BRIEFLY DESCRIBE YOUR IDEA

- o New products, services or sub-products;
- o new processes;
- o new business models;
- o new uses for existing products;
- o new markets and product developments;
- o new distribution channels;
- o a technical or scientific discovery.

WHAT VISION OF THE PRODUCT, MODEL, MARKET, DISTRIBUTION, SUB-PRODUCT, AND/OR SERVICE WILL YOU GENERATE WITH THIS IDEA?

- o You can use different channels of distribution for sub-products and /or general services;
- o strategies and short-term objectives (maximum 6-8 months) to develop, for maximum reach and to launch an innovation for an already established business;
- o development of a new market, intended for new consumers;
- o projection of low costs during the development;
- o innovation in quality for the service and presentation;
- o model of an application for a new market.

11

> WHAT COMBINATIONS CAN I MAKE WITH THIS NEW
> PRODUCT, PROCESS, MODEL, MARKET, SERVICE,
> DISTRIBUTION, OR SUB-PRODUCT?

- o Innovation of the product and commercialization of a new consumer specialty;
- o in an established business, products with a new talented and creative aspect;
- o combination of services and products;
- o new process combined with a model consisting of a variety of products and different distribution channels;
- o a new commercial model for artisanal products and sub-products;
- o combining or linking intelligence with customer service.

The second factor or element of the Imagery Representation Model is **where.** As represented in Figure 1.5, **where** do you place your idea geographically to establish a business? You will see the model for placement, type of client to target, and growth of the idea. In this phase, you will describe the placement of your idea geographically, in terms of deciding the best place for a successful and full exploitation of the representation.

Also, you should consider logistics and the market in local, regional, national, and international sectors. This should be consistent with the placement and the direction of the innovation that you are developing, so that the client or consumer can get the full advantage of the idea you generate and thus guarantee total success.

There is a possibility of starting a particular innovative idea in one place and ending up with a business in another city, region, or country. You must analyze certain specifications of the kind of business you are planning, studying the data and the location of the potential consumer for this type of innovative product, subproduct, or service. You should do an analysis of the type of consumer for your innovation, for which you will research logistical data that will identify a specific type, where your business can function successfully.

There are ideas that can be aimed at certain consumers in different fields, such as manufacturing, consulting, businesses in the primary sector or point of sale in strategic areas (airports, malls, metro stations, buses, trade fairs, catalogue sales, among others), which can be conducted on a personal computer on the internet. Remember to do this with creativity, intelligence, and enthusiasm. It is represented as follows.

Figure 1.5

Imagery Representation Model

TABLE 2

TO WHOM IS THIS IDEA DIRECTED?

STAR SOLVER

WHERE TO PLACE YOUR IDEA GEOGRAPHICALLY TO ESTABLISH A BUSINESS?

- Type of consumers: children, young people, adults, seniors, doctors, engineers, persons with disabilities, schools, among others.
- Products that are required by consumers for daily use.
- Aimed specifically at foreign nationals.
- Meant only for athletes.
- A new service in an innovative technology (solar energy).
- Exclusively for the government sector.
- Business in the beginning stages of selling products wholesale in local and regional areas.
- New process for developing a catalog of innovative products at an international level and advertised on the Internet.
- Services or products focused exclusively on gastronomy for a special type of consumer.
- Ideas for local products, exclusively sold to state or municipal governments.
- Ideas for natural organic products or sub-products and for protecting the environment.

WHERE DO YOU FIND CLIENTS OR CONSUMERS IN YOUR
CITY, STATE, COUNTRY, AND/OR INTERNATIONALLY?

- o Local, regional, national, and international trade fairs.
- o Finding consumers on the Internet (statistics data section or directly via individual consumers).
- o Commercial section of consular and embassy services.
- o Economic departments, business section, data and statistics, Institute of Business Statistics of your country.
- o Through advertising in specialized business magazines.

WILL YOU OPERATE A BUSINESS FROM A CENTRAL OFFICE:
ON THE INTERNET, WORD OF MOUTH, POINT OF SALE,
MANUFACTURER, OR SOMEWHERE ELSE?

- o In association or shared lease.
- o Mobile stand located where people gather.
- o Renting in community kitchens; renting in industrial spaces.
- o On the Internet or catalogue sales, among others.

The third factor or element of the Imagery Representation Model is **who**. As represented in Figure 1.6, **who** is the type of client, and what strategies are needed for teaming up at the beginning of this exercise? In this phase, you will begin thinking about the process of generating your idea, followed by the type of prospective client who would benefit from the idea for your venture. You will search out financial resources to support your innovation, and this book will guide you in finding and obtaining these types of local, state, federal, and international financial subsidies and from private organizations, among others.

You will decide what strategy to use and how to start using the funding to begin working on your innovation. At the same time, you will look into whether your innovative idea already exists in national or international markets, that is, you will look into technological improvements, accelerated development, protecting and patenting the idea, geographic indicators, among others.

You will also research the possibility of collaborating on projects with universities, startups, subsidiaries of philanthropic organizations, national networks of incubators, financial and business developers, angel investors, mixed funds, business development, funding for technological innovation, programs for entrepreneurs, programs for ideas, private foundations, participation and agreements with international collaborators, such as foreign governments that support projects based on innovative ideas, among others.

The third factor **who** and the sixth factor **how** relate to opening doors to funding opportunities for launching your innovation.

You will focus on the following information in your search for funding.

1. Types of projects of interest to the organization or financial entity that awards nonrefundable grants; an association, a foundation, an international organization, mixed funding, a university, among others.

2. The rules of engagement of each organization that grants funds or subsidies. When you submit a document or innovative project of interest to an organization, you should be aware of all the conditions that are specified and required.

3. Dates for submission of the final documentation.

4. Personal contact with the director of the area of the innovation of interest. Always maintain communication related to your innovation.

5. Format for submitting the final document or project (electronic, certified mail, in person, other specified formats).

6. Always inquire about the possibility of requesting two or more financial grants for the same project from different organizations.

There are other elements at play in this third factor of the model that you will have to carefully consider, such as focusing on who will be the main consumer of the results of your innovative idea. You will look for that ideal consumer as it relates to these two points.

- The image or attractiveness of your innovative product or service.

- The quality, service, value of innovation, and distribution of the product.

The image or attractiveness of the innovation that you create in your product, service, or result will go hand in hand with the uniqueness of the transformation with which you execute or implement that concept, which will catch the customer's eye with the beauty of the product and the quality of the service, distribution, or other new need that you identify.

In addition, your search for the potential client should be approached with an open mind, as it relates to the type of consumer (private companies, governments, persons with disabilities, senior citizens, young people, individuals with sophisticated and diverse ideas, in different levels of production).

There will be a symbiotic element between your innovative idea and the consumer, as long as you carry out your transformation with these four ideas.

1. Creativity and talent.

2. Added quality to the product or service.

3. Inventiveness and a new twist.

4. An excellent marketing strategy.

This way you will be able to continually innovate.

This third stage of the Imagery Representation Model includes the option of including a collaborator or participant. If you consider the need to associate and work with a team, you should keep in mind the specialty or experience of each of the participants, according to their areas of expertise. Alternatively, you can approach professional business consultants, found in research centers, chambers of commerce, universities, technology transfer centers, national incubator groups, and others, free of charge.

The model for this option is represented in Figure 1.6, where you will see the template mentioned above.

Figure 1.6

Imagery Representation Model

TABLE
3

| WHAT STRATEGY WILL YOU USE FOR TEAMING UP AT THE START OF YOUR IDEA? |

STAR SOLVER

WHO IS THE TYPE OF CLIENT AND WHAT STRATEGIES TO USE FOR TEAMING UP AT THE BEGINNING OF THIS IDEA?

- Identify and research funding at local, state, national, and international levels (private and governmental).
- Research the World Intellectual Property Organization (WIPO), The national registry of information technology and innovative ideas, and others on the Internet and in local or foreign libraries.
- Look for opportunities to associate with investors interested in your idea.
- General estimate of costs and market opportunities.
- Analysis of a general summary of your idea.

| WHO WILL BE THE TYPE OF CLIENT THAT WILL BUY THIS PRODUCT? |

- Make a list of consumers for each product, service, or result that you create with the innovation.
- Research different uses for your idea and then search out the type of consumer.
- Explore developments in innovation services with broad criteria for integration and intelligence.

| IS THERE A STRATEGY OR POSSIBILITY FOR CONDUCTING A PROFESSIONAL SURVEY FOR GROWING OR EXPANDING YOUR IDEA INTO A BUSINESS OPPORTUNITY? |

- Yes, or no, that is, for strengthening the concept and growing your business or organizational plan.

- There are centers in universities and international organizations that specialize in business development consulting free of charge.

19

The fourth factor or element of the Imagery Representation Method is **when.** As represented in Figure 1.7, **when** you launch, what kind of installations and operating systems do you need to turn that idea into a business? In this phase, you will specify your projected activities and functions sequentially, concisely, and in an orderly fashion from the moment you generate your idea with descriptions of the tasks relative to the times and dates of all the activities to the end. In addition, you will fully document the development and formation of all the activities of your idea. You will determine what those activities are based on their technical requirements.

You should chart a schedule for the proper management of your resources, total time, products or services, subproducts, new business models, markets, location of the clients, management strategies, and everything related to the implementation of your idea. Also, you should focus on the type of installations where you will carry out your innovation, along with its development and implementation.

To sum up, in this phase, you will list different approaches to the idea with a chart of activities to perform within a range of variables, focusing exclusively on the functionality and development of your original idea. You will indicate, in general terms, the management of your sequential plan and specific activities, the estimates of resources for the activities related to your general idea, and deadlines and time constraints for the functions.

Figure 1.7

Imagery Representation Model

TABLE 4

WHEN I LAUNCH, WHAT KIND OF INSTALLATIONS AND OPERATING SYSTEM DO I NEED TO TURN THAT IDEA INTO A BUSINESS?

WHEN WILL I INITIATE MY IDEA FOR A BUSINESS AND/OR SERVICE?

STAR SOLVER

- Make a list of activities in the plan and prioritize them.
- You start your business at the moment you put your idea on paper to turn it into a project.
- State your objectives and short-term goals, and carry them through to completion.
- Use your agenda and get organized.

WHAT PERMITS OR AUTHORIZATIONS DO I NEED (CITY, STATE, FEDERAL, AND/OR INTERNATIONAL) FOR TURNING MY IDEA INTO AN INNOVATIVE BUSINESS?

- Information about permits and licenses needed for the innovation project.
- Do not forget to look into patenting or protecting your idea, you could register it as a trademark.
- Permits for starting a business.
- You could contemplate starting an innovation project in a university incubator as a step in Phase 0.

WHAT KIND OF INSTALLATIONS DO I NEED FOR TURNING MY INNOVATIVE IDEA INTO A BUSINESS?

- I could start it in an incubator for ideas or at a center for entrepreneurs.
- University laboratory.
- In your garage, in the first stages of the innovation.
- A leasing agreement in an industrial space, a store, restaurant, warehouse, laboratory, etcetera.
- High-tech centers.

21

The fifth factor or element in the Imagery Representation Model is **why**. As represented in Figure 1.8, **why** will your idea relate to the client? Here you will analyze the functions of the most important activities in terms of the following questions.

- Why are you creating or developing the idea?

- What motivates or inspires you to develop the innovation?

- In what way will it benefit the consumer?

- What endorsement is needed for the service, product, or invention that you will create for your clients? These clients could be direct or indirect, regular or occasional, wholesalers or retailers, among others.

You will also list the skills you will use to attract new consumers to your concept. You will create advertising and commercial opportunities during the innovation process, as there will be occasions to attract consumers. That is, during the process of transformation, experimentation, and innovation, there are opportunities to interact with clients, which will let you take full advantage of the entire innovation process until you arrive at the final product or result.

The contacts and information generated during the process of developing an innovation are important commercially, because you want to take advantage of the publicity needed to make your abilities and cleverness known during the innovation process.

You will establish short-term and long-term objectives where you will carry out those tasks while observing important aspects of your innovation, while developing and implementing the strategies that you design and propose. This way you will complete your cycle of innovation when you ask yourself why your idea will relate to your customer, devise a commercial framework, detect potential economic areas, and lay out the creation of your innovation product, service, or result that you plan to achieve. The main idea should strongly appeal to the consumer for its quality, innovative value, or simply for the improved function of the new product or service compared to other competitors.

Figure 1.8

Imagery Representation Model

TABLE 5

HOW DO I INTEREST CONSUMERS AND CLIENTS IN MY IDEA?

STAR SOLVER

WHY WILL MY IDEA RELATE TO THE CLIENT?

○ It should be a new and clever innovation.
○ Always top quality and customer service.
○ Remember, when implementing your innovation
  always protect the environment and everything related to it.
○ Product innovation involves a healthy and productive competition.
○ Innovation in the form of educational and promotional transition.
○ Price consistent with the value of innovation, better quality, and transformative logistics.

WHY AM I CREATING THIS IDEA FOR MY CLIENTS?

○ Intelligence, broad vision, intuition, experience, creativity, talent, motivation, needs of the consumer, and inventiveness.
○ Related to my ability, technique, scientific specialty, or it is my profession.
○ Aptitude and specialized ability.

WHY ARE CLIENTS GOING TO BUY MY PRODUCT?

- o   Better quality, innovation, and service.
- o   Competitive innovative value.
- o   It is unique to the market.
- o   Daily need of consumers.

WHAT STRATEGY WILL I USE TO PROMOTE MY IDEA TO MY CLIENTS?

- o   Innovative marketing and product.
- o   Short term strategy, and if needs to be extended you should explain why.
- o   Packaging of the innovative product: new design to improve your product presentation.
- o   New technological tools for the development of your product.

The sixth factor or element of the Imagery Representation Model is **how.** As represented in Figure 1.9, **how** do you begin to exploit your innovative idea financially to start a business? This is the last factor for you to consider in the promotional, incentive, and comparative analysis of any financial system to raise the level of research and development conducted by technical, professional, and other skilled personnel. After generating this great idea, you will ask where you can find the capital to get started on your innovation. With this question, you will put into motion a search for funding, in your home country or abroad.

There are organizations and governments in various countries that earmark money specifically for innovative ideas in different fields. You will use these incentives, subsidies, and funding for developing, organizing, and planning, according to the deadlines stipulated for submitting documents and updating the main aspects of the plan, to compete for and thus secure the necessary funding for developing your innovation.

Where do you look for the capital or economic incentives to be able to start your first phase or cycle of innovation? And during the consulting-and-research stage, how do you find those organizations and funding to carry out projects like yours? To obtain this capital or funding through open competition for entrepreneurial projects, you will always need to have a final document that conforms to the requirements stipulated by the specific organization showing the stages of the innovation project. In the vast field of innovation, you can find different levels of funding or incentives through national and international private and government organizations, programs for entrepreneurs, business incubators for innovative ideas and projects, pre-accelerators, venture capitalists, angel investors, banks, universities, or mentors who fund innovative projects, among others.

The final document that you create while working on your innovation should have no more than sixteen pages and be based on a template with the specific format required by the organization. Usually, organizations take about six months to review such a document and to announce the winning projects in the competition.

Figure 1.9

Imagery Representation Model

TABLE 6

FINANCING MY IDEA TO TRANSFORM INTO A BUSINESS.

STAR SOLVER

o Your idea in a final document or a project seventy per cent completed.
o List of organizations where you can submit your project for review and to open competitions for funding.
o Always stay in contact with the person responsible for reviewing projects.
o List all the organizations where you apply for or receive funding from in the project application.

WHERE CAN I FIND NON-REIMBURSABLE FINANCIAL SUPPORT (SUBSIDIES) TO START MY INNOVATION?

o Subsidies from local, state, and federal governments, private organizations, philanthropic groups, consulates and embassies, programs from entrepreneurial groups, venture capitalists, angel investors, business innovation accelerator and pre-accelerator programs, entrepreneurial universities, incubators, banking institutions, funding and incentives for innovation, etc.
o Specify the main qualities of your idea in the specific area of interest. Doing this will make it easier to find subsidies related to your innovation.

HOW DO I BEGIN TO EXPLOIT MY INNOVATION IDEA FINANCIALLY TO START A BUSINESS?

> **HOW DOES A NON-REIMBURSABLE SUBSIDY OR INCENTIVE WORK DURING THE INNOVATION?**

- o Research areas of innovation that are of interest to organizations granting subsidies.
- o Finalize the plan for your idea in a document of no more than 16-19 pages. Submit the project on the specified date.
- o Always follow a template for the description of your project.
- o Time for document review will be about 6 months, depending on the type of organization.
- o There are usually four phases of study during the innovation process.
  (Phase 0. Justification for the innovation study).
  (Phase 1. Experimentation).
  (Phase 2. Commercialization).
  (Phase 3. Opening the establishment or business).
- o Different types of subsidies are awarded by the granting organization for each phase.

> **HOW MUCH MONEY IS USUALLY AWARDED AS NON-REIMBURSABLE SUBSIDIES OR INCENTIVES?**

- o The average subsidies or incentives range from $5,000 to $100,000.
- o The amount usually depends on the area of innovation and/or the funds available from the sponsoring organization, state, or country.

What If You Do Not Like What You See in Your Idea?

It is possible that you will not like what you see, learn, or uncover about your idea. If this is the case, change it. Imagine it as you would like it to be, and ask yourself the following.

How would you like things to be when you implement the changes?

What would be the best possible result from making the changes?

What products, services, or results would you like to add to that picture for a better outcome?

Why will consumers want to buy those new products or services? Look at each one of them separately, if you have more than one product or service.

Why do you want to change those products or services?

Visualize your ideas for the new products or services. Think about how you are going to implement the process of innovating the concept or idea.

What would that innovation be like? Record all the answers you come up with. Be specific, clear, and objective.

What would you do?

What would your plan be?

Will you need to meet with a consultant, university researcher, or particular advisor in your area of interest?

Do you need training in a particular material or specific aspect of your idea?

Are there subsidies or nonreimbursable funds for the training that you might need?

Will it take a long time to make these changes?

These are some of the questions you might ask yourself if you are not happy with what you have at this moment. If you do not like what you see, there is a possibility of combining that idea with others and then carry your project to completion.

With this, the chapter finishes on visualizing the potential of an idea. In Chapter 2, I will address the process of organizing the idea. In addition, you will work on conceptualizing what you have learned to make full use of your great idea and develop an effective innovation process to create a clear and intelligent concept.

SECTION 2
ORGANIZATION

The organizational phase of the idea involves developing the structural configuration with its extensions, which becomes the blueprint showing the project broken down, including additional variables. These variables represent alternatives intended to support the main idea. Included in this organizational and thought-provoking blueprint are order, distribution, skills, uses, techniques, and discoveries of new elements that have the potential of improving the main action and contributing to the further development of the idea.

Also, in the process you will generate a series of data needed during the development phase that will help you create a presentation document from the idea's brief. This document will be the concrete basis for your innovative idea that could be submitted to any organization that might help you with funds or financial assistance to take your innovation process to fruition. There should also be an abridged presentation document of your idea to show to any organization that you might wish to approach.

CHAPTER 2
ORGANIZING AN IDEA

The process of organizing an idea consists of breaking down the concept, thought, or knowledge that you are considering into steps; laying them out in order as an overview; and allowing the feedback that emerges from the basic elements to surface to allow you to take full advantage of the original idea that you wish to develop or apply. You should carry out this process of breaking down the idea by highlighting the main element of the concept that resulted from your creative, analytical, and research activities, and channeling that information and the additional answers or discoveries you might make to the central action, thus complementing the idea.

You can do this using small subgroups or clusters that you turn into new, relevant contributions that can help you achieve a better composition, integration, operation, systematization, and configuration of all the components present in the body of the original idea. Also, by adding input, you are contributing to the improvement of the layout for the final concept. The main objectives or benefits resulting from this process are the following.

1. Breaking down of the context to generate feedback for the idea.

2. Optimum summarization of all the uses of the resulting idea.

3. Projection of the results with wide vision and interpretation.

4. Addition of the components required to be competitive in the application of your innovation, price accessibility, production cost profitability, and for carrying out the observation and analysis of barriers that might hamper the process of creating the idea.

5. Presentation of simple operational strategies for the main central action that is being developed in the course of the innovation process.

Applying this process will help you enhance the ability to expand and measure what you intend or want to fulfill. In addition, during the production process, you will become aware of the outcome of the principal action and how well it is developed in terms of its dynamic, which is an important factor when innovating and formulating a final idea.

You should approach this organizational phase by keeping the big picture in mind while focusing on the elements of the idea's main action, using well-founded criteria. These criteria should include a series of data and factors that will help you see the best order, support, outcomes, and configuration of the peripheral elements that surround your original idea. That way you will be able to take full advantage of the constructive information that can enhance your initial idea by way of useful feedback that results from the process.

Represented in Figure 2.1 are the components that result from implementing the process of organizing an idea. The goal of this representation is to generate results for the innovation concept, creating feedback loops that interact with elements of the original idea. This way your idea will grow to its full potential and, together with other elements, create an overview of the concept, documentation, and data of your blueprint and information. Also, using this technique will maximize the effective range of the innovation of the product, service, or result that you are working on. At this stage, you will begin the process of breaking down the original idea that you generated into steps.

The process begins with the data input, which is the phase where you analyze and describe the main goal of the original idea. You will continue with a series of tools and techniques that might play an active role in the development of the process of breaking down the main idea during the operationalization phase. Finally, you will integrate all this in a series of reconstructions and outlines that will help you consolidate all the proposed information to implement the innovation, in such way that every factor present will generate data output that will help shape the final idea. This way you will end up with a draft of the full, updated, verified, and documented concept, which is the end product of the process of illustrating your idea and its components.

Figure 2.1

Components That Form Part of the Process of Organizing an Idea

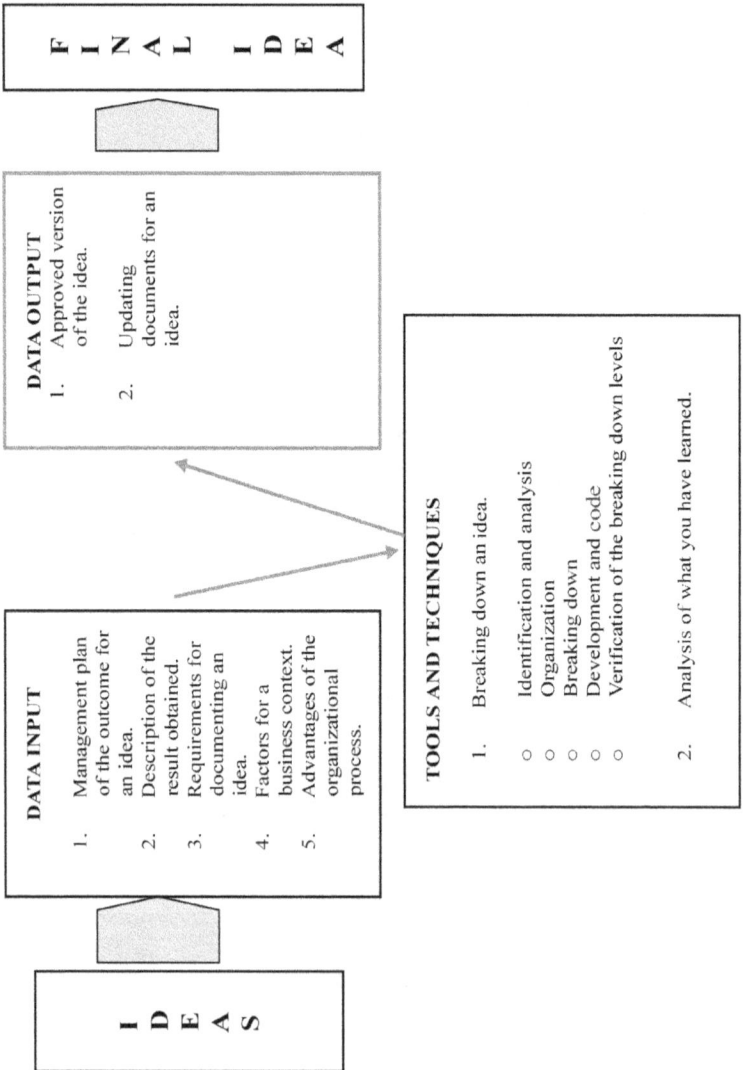

FINAL IDEA

DATA OUTPUT

1. Approved version of the idea.

2. Updating documents for an idea.

DATA INPUT

1. Management plan of the outcome for an idea.
2. Description of the result obtained.
3. Requirements for documenting an idea.
4. Factors for a business context.
5. Advantages of the organizational process.

TOOLS AND TECHNIQUES

1. Breaking down an idea.

   ○ Identification and analysis
   ○ Organization
   ○ Breaking down
   ○ Development and code
   ○ Verification of the breaking down levels

2. Analysis of what you have learned.

IDEAS

Data Entry

Below, you will find a description of how to organize the data input and its steps for the process of organizing an idea, which begins with the following step.

1. **Management plan of the outcome for an idea.**
   This is the first step in the data input process, where you specify, briefly and concisely, in a single line, the description of the process for the use, application, and main action of the activity while developing that original idea, always keeping in mind the specific area (product, service, or vision) for which you intend to deliver innovative, transformative, and original results. This way you will find out how to be efficient in the implementation of the operation, which is the main objective of the process of innovating.

2. **Description of the result obtained.**
   In this step, you will specify the most important and unique characteristics, clearly detailing the results from the central idea, specific function, or prototype in the representation that you plan to launch. You should conduct a descriptive analysis of what you wish to accomplish during the innovation process, indicating all the elements in terms of their use, service, distribution, and in a new light, based on the outline of your final idea.

   You might classify this as a service, distribution, or some other aspect of a primary, secondary, or tertiary economic sector. It should be presented as an idea that is actively being developed, specifying what makes the main idea different from that of your competitors and making comparisons if needed.

3. **Requirements for documenting an idea.**
   This step outlines the type of information or documentation that you need to generate from your research, which is

necessary for understanding your results, and for developing your idea. In addition, during the development process, you will need more information to be able to appreciate the scope of the idea for your product, service, or result. This requires researching historic and practical precedents related to the main concept of your original idea.

4. **Factors for a business context.**
This is the step where you outline the specifics of the industrial sector that could benefit from your original idea, based on its main aspects, which will help you identify the most relevant characteristics. You will also be able to think about the tools that will be needed for developing the concept for your idea, which will culminate in a successful research portfolio for a business or for a school project about innovation. Also, this phase will include a variety of sources, which will help you form a plan or configure an idea.

The type of industry will determine how to organize the idea in a way that is relevant to the nature of the concept. In addition, this can be helpful because it lets you use external sources as inspiration for generating ideas. For example, for an engineering idea, you might refer to the section on creative systems in the processes and uses division of the International Organization for Standardization (IOS), which can help you develop new ideas that might result in innovation projects.

5. **Advantages of the organizational process.**
This section outlines the conditions and advantages of organizing an original idea, which can influence the creative configuration of the development process, the scope of the proposal, new additions, and communication during the idea's structuring phase. This organizational process includes the following elements.

- Procedures, policies, and templates for organizing an idea.

- Documenting data related to preliminary concepts linked to representations stemming from the main action.

- Learning from previous ideas.

Tools and Techniques

The steps in the process of organizing an idea in the section of tools and techniques, which is where the hierarchical process is implemented, are as follows.

1. **Breaking down an idea.**
    The process of breaking down an idea, represented in Figure 2.2, is a technique used to divide and subdivide activities that provide feedback and that project the main action, to integrate them in the most creative way to achieve growth in the innovation and attain the desired results. The purpose of this step is to create greater reach and integration of the original idea that you generate during its development process.

    This is an important technique, which is needed to support the core idea and to bring it to fruition. You will break down the system into small fragments or sections that identify the objectives that need to be implemented, with improvements that are incorporated to ensure proper functionality, integration, and management resulting from this representation, concept, or idea. The breaking down of an idea must be carried out in an orderly fashion in small work units.

    These work units are arranged in descending order during the development and configuration process. You might include generalizations in the planning and valuation of the idea if you consider it appropriate. This will help you focus closely on the process of structuring the idea.

The breaking down process should always be done deliberately and with control, keeping in mind the results that stem from the main action, because in the process of implementing your innovation, you will end up with several drafts that will help you advance toward the results. The degree of detail in the work units will vary according to the breadth and complexity of the idea that you are working on, because an idea can have a multitude and variety of levels. Generally, the following activities are included when you proceed to break down an idea.

- Identification and analysis of a single product or result with the potential of becoming a service that can be turned into a final idea. This way you will be able to establish a solid foundation for a business or for a school project about innovation.

- Organization, order, and configuration of the process for breaking down an idea.

- Breaking down earlier, at the beginning of the process of structuring the idea. This could be organized by development, importance, reasoning, or by some type of engineering that can be used to manage the general idea.

- Development and code assignment of a system for the identification of every element in the process of the idea's organization.

- Verification of the breaking down levels of deconstruction of the product, result, or service that you are focusing on, whenever a determination, mechanism, and basic instrumentation is required to produce and bring a final idea to fruition.

Figure 2.2

Example of the Hierarchical Deconstruction of an Idea into Small Tasks Represented by Descending Branches to Achieve Maximum Efficiency

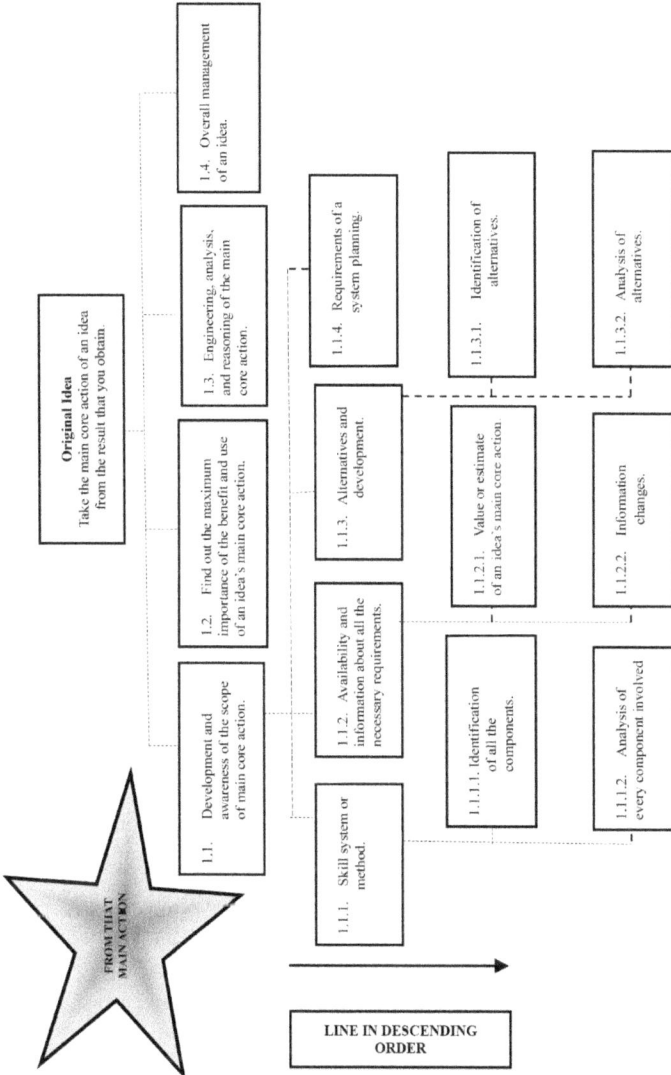

Original Idea
Take the main core action of an idea from the result that you obtain.

1.1. Development and awareness of the scope of main core action.

1.2. Find out the maximum importance of the benefit and use of an idea's main core action.

1.3. Engineering, analysis, and reasoning of the main core action.

1.4. Overall management of an idea.

1.1.1. Skill system or method.

1.1.2. Availability and information about all the necessary requirements.

1.1.3. Alternatives and development.

1.1.4. Requirements of a system planning.

1.1.1.1. Identification of all the components.

1.1.1.2. Analysis of every component involved

1.1.2.1. Value or estimate of an idea's main core action

1.1.2.2. Information changes.

1.1.3.1. Identification of alternatives.

1.1.3.2. Analysis of alternatives.

FROM THAT MAIN ACTION

LINE IN DESCENDING ORDER

In this hierarchical, descending deconstruction process you will be able to establish windows of opportunity for a main action and thus introduce ideas and technical elements that strengthen the process and all the requirements needed to complete the configuration of an idea. These elements can result from the feedback for the main action, which can be the following.

- Knowing the limits and full scope of the action.

- Documenting mainly the use or quality.

- Information, analysis, and basis for the action.

- Overall administration and global direction of the idea.

You will be able to follow its ramifications until you complete the identification of every element, the benefits, and the description of the analysis to be able to organize your idea.

2. Analysis of what you have learned.
   This exercise is commonly used during the idea's breaking down or deconstruction process to determine the meaning of any verified information that forms an integral part of the main action. You should lay this out in analytical increments for any information or ability required for the development of the documentation of a service needed to complete the idea's process, projection, or productive phase.

During the development of the tools and techniques phase, the deconstruction process is carried out through creative actions and knowledge analysis. The experience factor of the main action comes into play in the technical details and is what drives the development of an idea, which is important.

Also, knowledge is delivered by any group or individual with functional skills that can be turned into similar ideas or for similar areas of business. In addition, you will be able to use predefined templates to organize ideas that have the potential to become a product, service, process, market, subproduct, distribution channel, or other area of development that you wish to pursue.

The templates, already predefined, can be classified by industry or by specific discipline or experience for the idea being developed. The person generating the idea will be able to determine the concept's final breakdown process by dividing it into work units that can be used for editing, testing effectiveness, and defining a process to manage the main idea.

The Process of Organizing an Idea Can Be Carried Out in Two Ways

1. **Method of descending order.**
   This process for organizing an idea is initially done in descending order, from top to bottom. It is a guided method that helps you organize and specify the development and innovation of the structure or configuration of a product, service, or result that you obtain from the main idea. Also, you will be able to use it for guidance, as a template, to easily create the deconstruction system, for analysis, and identification of how to strengthen your idea.

2. **Method of ascending order.**
   This process for structuring an idea is initially done in ascending order, from bottom to top. Included in this method are all the subcomponents of the product, resulting from the development of the structure during the breaking down or deconstruction process.

The representation of an idea's structuring process stems from the main action and from any result obtained from the original idea to provide feedback that includes variables, which will help enhance the innovation and arrive at the definitive idea. This process is outlined as follows.

- Building and utilizing new facets of the life cycle of the original idea. These facets are broken down by levels, which help maximize the information. The levels can be secondary, tertiary, or beyond and will present creative concepts, alternative channels for development and research, and allow you to use them as integral elements, which is essential for the development of the main action and the enhancement of the idea.

- Incorporating alternatives in the last stages of the deconstruction process during the evolution of the development of the main action. This includes the use of tools for the new components of the innovation that you introduce for the expansion and information of the scope of the main action, which will be used as the basis for the original idea.

During this process of deconstructing the idea you will be able to include stages or levels that incorporate subcomponents that include elements aimed at organizations or companies interested in your original idea. You might be able to turn a main action into an idea through contracts or work orders, where you can specify the type of business alliance or agreement of the concept proposals that you receive. There are confidentiality clauses that require mutual agreement for the process—for example, the development and inclusion of the sale of an idea, support and understanding memoranda for the structuring process of an idea for organizations—for creative undertakings or for large industry.

Throughout this system you will include detailed descriptions of all your innovation's specifications in terms of its innovative value and the evolution of the main central action. The breaking down of the components into levels at the early stages of the structuring process requires subdividing the functions of the results generated from the main action. You should include the subcomponents as essential elements of a product, process, model, subproduct, market, or main component of an idea's action.

The configuration of the process can be represented as a plan for systematization and coordination, together with the descending and ascending layout, because it is at this stage that you can see the hierarchical stages of the deconstructed components. This process will help determine whether the lower stages of the organigram for the implementation of an idea are necessary and if they contribute to the completion of the definitive and final idea.

Data Output

Described below is the last component of the structuring process of an idea, the data output, which is part of the last phase of the development, and it includes two elements.

1. **Approved version of the idea.**
   The basic factor of a finalized model encompasses the aggregate of the products, services, or results, which together form the action and function plan for the main component and constitute the final idea. This final model should include procedures that take into account the changes that could take place and that could be used as a comparison tool. This step is an integral component of the management plan of any idea, and includes the following elements.

   • Central premise of an idea. The central description of the idea's functional activity created and directed toward the product, result, or ability to perform a needed service, with results to carry out and complete the project for an idea.

   • Structural processing of the idea. An orderly deconstruction of all the products, services, and results generated from your idea. Using this as feedback, you will be able to construct a clear diagram. Each descending level should be represented by a specific strategy that supports the main idea. The idea's structural process is finalized when the work units are arranged to have better control and thus establish an individual specific activity for the idea. These work units provide a hierarchical summative structure of costs, planning, and of all the idea's existing resources.

2. Updating documents for an idea.
This refers to an efficient, updated document for an idea, where you will include all the requirements that form part of the document with room for potential updates or improvements. This way you will have a reference during its approval-and-authorization process when you make any changes or updates. You will be able to use it as a proposal during the idea's structuring process.

Flow Chart for the Creation of Your Presentation Document

When the data output is incorporated, you can consider the organizational process of the idea completed. You have transformed the original idea into an orderly and thorough blueprint of your final concept or representation. This signals the completion of the design of an active idea, structured and ready to be diagrammed as a flow chart, which is represented in Figure 2.3, that can be transferred to a manuscript called the presentation document. In this document, which represents your idea, you will include the basic results described in the diagram, which will consist of six key points from the draft.

In this brief and concise manuscript, you will lay out your idea in no more than three pages, where you will describe your active final innovative concept. This document will be the presentation of your innovative idea for any agency or organization where you might be soliciting support or funds, nonrefundable financing or subsidies, with the goal of putting this innovation into motion.

In the first meetings or inquiries made to any organization, bank, university, or state agency, to name a few, this presentation document will be the first introduction document that you will provide. It will be proof of your interest in an intelligent idea that can be applied to an innovative area of your expertise. The agency or organization where you apply for financial assistance will respond and deliver acknowledgment, in writing, of receipt of your presentation document and will notify you of their decision of whether they are interested in your idea or not.

The diagram or the flow chart is not intended to overwhelm you with research prospects and documents, but rather its purpose is to provide the best basic productive and descriptive information about the idea that you would like to develop and to transform it into an innovative project in a concise, effective, and well-documented manner that you can later present to an agency or organization to request funds and as a way to convey information about your idea so it can be taken to fruition. This way you will detail your experimental design for the creation of your product, service, or result using the best description of the following points, which you should include in the presentation document.

- **Knowledge of the background of the innovative idea.** In this section, you will detail the history of your idea throughout the innovation process. You will identify the problem that you intend to solve, including the innovative aspect that you will implement, briefly discussing the nature of the problem and the statistical data that resulted from your research.

- **Development of a plan and direction for your idea.** You will describe the proposed product that you intend to develop, in general terms, including objectives that you are experimenting with. You will complement it with a brief outline of the development and direction of that great innovative idea that you are proposing with its analysis and experimental design, which outlines that innovation during the development process.

- **Outline of activities and their planning.** This consists of laying out concisely the general approach for the activities that you will develop to carry out that innovation, detailing the starting and ending dates, the activities undertaken, and an estimation of the time to complete them.

- **Identification of the risks and the scope of the project during the innovation phase.** Here you will briefly mention the foreseeable technical risks and the way you intend to tackle those contingencies during the innovation process. In addition, you will sum up the overall scope of the innovation project.

- **Location and cost estimates.** You will identify the appropriate locations and facilities where the innovation will be carried out, as well as the total estimated cost to accomplish it. You should not detail equipment, salaries, leases, or other data that form part of the innovation's production process.

- **Members of the team and references.** Here you will develop a list of the members or advisors in your team and the references used in the creation of the presentation document.

When you create your data flow chart you will have to research the following four areas to obtain the descriptive points for your presentation document. You will carry them out in your research plan.

1. Administrative description and guide to the sum of products, results, or ability to carry out a service that is required for a smart final idea.

2. Activities and results of an innovation with calendar dates and estimated times for their completion.

3. Summary of documents required for the opening of the business and/or project undertaken.

4. Validation of the sum of products, services, and/or results that are obtained with their analysis and identification risks.

These descriptive points will help the managers of the organizations or agencies that you approach for financial assistance visualize the concept or idea that you plan to develop. This will become the first document that you will present in the way of professional presentation of the idea that you wish to accomplish.

Figure 2.3

Flow Chart of the Process

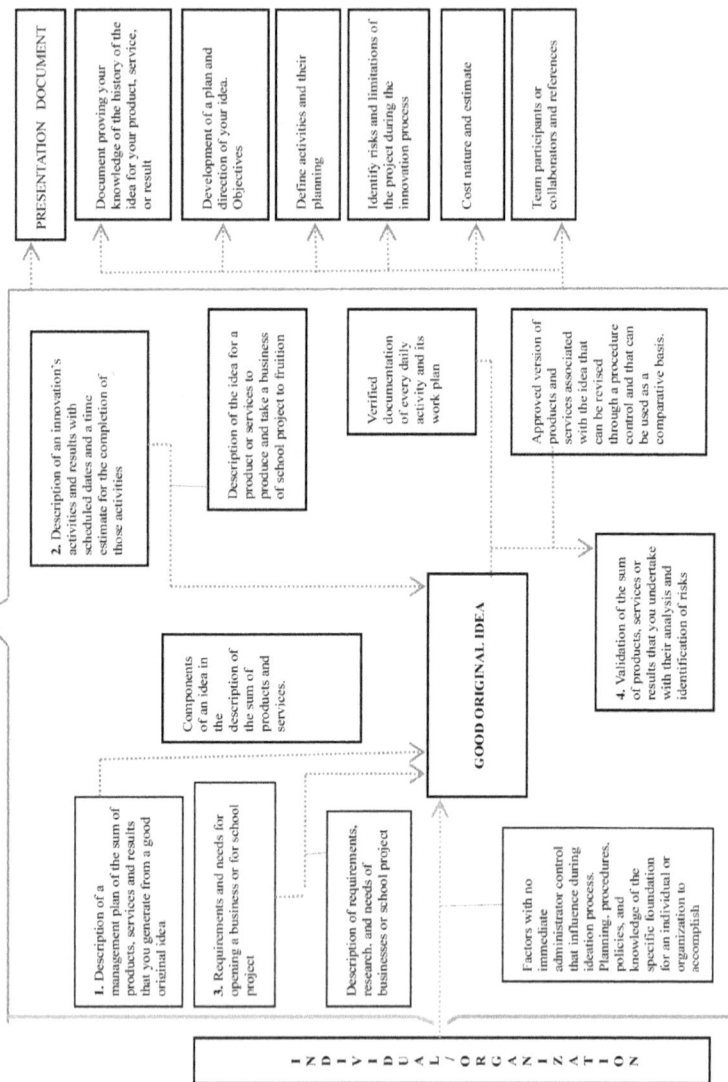

PRESENTATION DOCUMENT

Document proving your knowledge of the history of the idea for your product, service, or result

Development of a plan and direction of your idea. Objectives

Define activities and their planning

Identify risks and limitations of the project during the innovation process

Cost nature and estimate

Team participants or collaborations and references

2. Description of an innovation's activities and results with scheduled dates and a time estimate for the completion of those activities

Description of the idea for a product or services to produce and take a business of school project to fruition

Verified documentation of every daily activity and its work plan

Approved version of products and services associated with the idea that can be revised through a procedure control and that can be used as a comparative basis.

Components of an idea in the description of the sum of products and services.

GOOD ORIGINAL IDEA

4. Validation of the sum of products, services or results that you undertake with their analysis and identification of risks

1. Description of a management plan of the sum of products, services and results that you generate from a good original idea

3. Requirements and needs for opening a business or for school project

Description of requirements, research, and needs of businesses or school project

Factors with no immediate administrator control that influence during ideation process. Planning, procedures, policies, and knowledge of the specific foundation for an individual or organization to accomplish

INDIVIDUAL / ORGANIZATION

When you create the data flow chart of the process and its components, you will be generating the necessary data to complete the presentation document, which will help you convey your innovative idea to any institution that grants financial assistance for innovative projects in a comprehensive way, and turn this into the presentation of your final entrepreneurial idea.

SECTION 3
RESEARCH

ow you start the process of researching and laying out the most basic characteristics of the final idea's main action. To accomplish this, you will begin your research using the scientific method. The purpose of this method is to enhance your knowledge by utilizing concepts and hypotheses related to applications of technical, professional, and scientific innovations that you set out to accomplish.

You will conduct your research in a historic, descriptive, and experimental context, which will be key in every transformative aspect that is applied to innovation. This will teach you how to organize the data that you extract from your research using the format of a technical-scientific document to lay out the practical skills needed for a specialization or ability for the area that you develop. Furthermore, you will be able to use it to innovate or for a school assignment in a technological area or system that you decide to undertake.

CHAPTER 3

RESEARCH AND PROTOTYPE OF A FINAL TECHNICAL-SCIENTIFIC DOCUMENT FOR INNOVATION

Y ou will begin the research and development phase for your final document starting with a clear and concise representation. This research should be based on the main element of your idea, which will become the product, service, or result that you wish to develop. Your innovation will involve a specific concept, which you are going to transform and that you have developed during the idea's organizational phase described in the previous chapter.

The research begins by laying out technical, professional, and scientific aspects of the proposed topic or problem, which set the parameters for exploration with its boundaries and with elements that are relevant to that representation. The purpose of the research is to discover principles, procedures, and knowledge of what is feasible and the limitations of the scope of your idea at the conversion phase, when you are ready to activate your innovation. Having these data will give you reliable, verifiable, accurate, and applicable information in terms of knowledge surrounding your concept and the specific results that are generated.

There are two elements at play during the investigative process.
1. The process element.
2. The formal element.

The process element formulates how to carry out research of the problem being investigated. That is, it points to the steps needed to follow during the scientific method phase when you are searching for information about how to carry out an innovation. This includes a formal element, which indicates how to present the results during both the research phase and the conclusion phase, the latter being the final report of the investigation.

In this chapter, you will learn how the process and the time you invest in the development of a quality idea, and the application of the research method, are truly essential and valuable to do the following.

- Improve a system.

- Improve products.

- Improve existing markets.

- Improve uses.

- Improve earnings.

- Improve savings.

- Improve science.

- Create a better vision of the innovation.

In this way you will be pleased and inspired to envision the progression of the method and to follow its components to uncover new knowledge and be able to apply a scientific method. Do not be intimidated by the term *scientific*. You will be using a simple, basic, easy-to-use procedure, designed either for a technical and professional discipline or for completing a school project that will help you turn your exercise into innovation.

You will become familiar with the scientific method and its main elements, and, as you begin your research, you will come to appreciate this unique system that ensures the correct application of the process of doing research, as represented in Figure 3.1.

Figure 3.1

Scientific Method

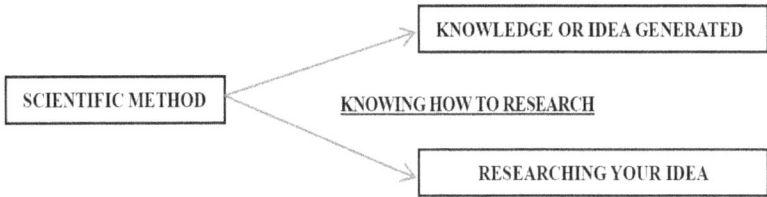

Additionally, this chapter shows you how to carry out research based on a solid foundation, beginning with learning about the scientific method.

The Scientific Method, a Simple Way to Research

The term *method* comes from the Greek *methodos* (road or pathway) and refers to the path used to achieve a goal. The scientific method is a process for discovering the conditions under which specific events happen, generally characterized as being experiments or tests, and verifiable through precise reasoning and empirical observation. It is the sum of the techniques and procedures that are used to advance knowledge.

The development and the use of the scientific method and the creative processes have evolved over the ages. They date their origins to ancient times, where scientific inventions included those of the Aztec culture that developed hydroponics (an agrarian technology), the Inca culture and their construction engineering, and the Mayan culture with their development of complex writing systems and astrology, among others.

In the area of methodology, we can go from the period of 427–345 BCE, with the Greek philosopher Plato, to the Egyptian text (1500 BCE) known as the Edwin Smith Papyrus, with its research in the medical field. One cannot talk about scientific methodology without mentioning the philosopher Aristotle, who made important contributions to the scientific tradition. Finally, during the Middle Ages, the issues that were addressed are what we refer to as science today.

There was greater theoretical and practical activity in the Islamic world than there was in classical periods, and the existence of science scholars, who could also be considered artisans, was common. Islamic scientific thinkers were often expert makers of instruments that helped improve the ability to make observations and calculations. Worth mentioning is the Islamic physicist Jabir Ibn Haytham (965-1039 BCE), who used experimentation and mathematics to produce results for his book on optics. The scientific methodology developed by Haytham consisted of the following steps.

1. Explicit statement of the problem subject to observation and to be tested through experimentation.

2. Research and/or review of a hypothesis using experimentation.

3. Interpretation of data and formulation of a conclusion using mathematical tools.

4. Publication and results.

We could provide a long list of inventors and scientists who contributed to the development of the scientific method. The history of technology is the history of the invention of tools and techniques with a practical purpose. Modern history is tightly linked to past scientific achievements, because it is the advancement of new understanding that has allowed us to create new tools that reciprocally have made possible new scientific and technological inventions, thanks to the development of new technologies, which have expanded the potential for experimentation and the acquisition of knowledge.

Elements of the Scientific Method

The elements of the scientific method are divided into two parts: concepts and hypothesis.

Concepts

Science investigates aspects of reality and reports its findings, and each area of science has its own terminology or concepts. From that we can say that any type of science presents a conceptual system. The concepts are logical structures created from intuitive impressions or perceptions and acquired experiences. These concepts have significance within a frame of reference.

Scientific concepts have to be reportable and conform to their own characteristics. Therefore, every project administrator should possess an expert vocabulary in the area of interest that is suitable for the understanding of the conceptual development and that is in line with the activities involved. You should use precise terminology, because this is essential for communication in writing about any project and easy to understand for the person who reviews the plan or project that you are developing.

Hypothesis

Hypotheses are indicators of what we are looking for within a realistic idea. A hypothesis is a proposition that can be tested to determine its validity. It always includes experimental or practical evidence; it is a question formulated in such way that it could anticipate an answer of some kind. Within the realm of hypotheses, concepts should be clearly defined. Every operation and prediction should be clearly expressed in a specific, rather than general, way. In addition, when you generate a hypothesis, it should be related to available techniques, so it can be subjected to tests or inquiry.

Applying the Scientific Method

Every project leader uses the scientific method to solve different types of problems. Scientists, technicians, and students who work on innovative projects use this methodology to achieve change by looking beyond to innovate a new product, service, and/or result that they wish to undertake in a particular field of development.

In your search for new knowledge, this process and scientific method is a useful tool for making use of that information to be able to effect innovation in any field of the modern world. The terms *technique, science,* and *technology* often blend together when they are used during this process.

Technology and science cause changes in production methods, way of life, and in many basic aspects of society. Science also affects culture and the general way in which societies think and behave, as represented in Figure 3.2.

Technique has referred, from the beginning, to the production of elements or objects that have a function, to the ability to make things. In time, the ability to make things becomes complex, which causes the emergence and development of technologists, as represented in Figure 3.2.

Figure 3.2

Technique—Technology and Science

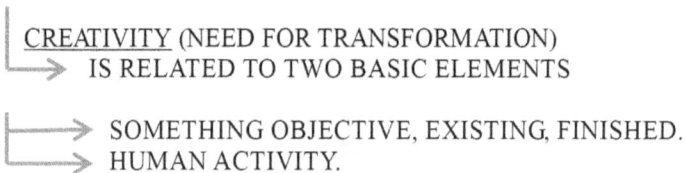

CREATIVITY (NEED FOR TRANSFORMATION)
→ IS RELATED TO TWO BASIC ELEMENTS

→ SOMETHING OBJECTIVE, EXISTING, FINISHED.
→ HUMAN ACTIVITY.

A technologist—the person who knows the how and why of things in specific areas and where there are relationships between technique, science, and knowledge—is where the term *technology* originates. Technology, in its wider sense of the term, is defined as the knowledge of a technique, the function of intelligence, of how to do things with a scientific method.

Science refers exclusively to the process of generating new knowledge through research. We might deduce that technique, science, and technology are differentiated by the different objectives they pursue. Technique and technology look for the application of the knowledge of how to do things to satisfy human needs. Science tries to understand nature and society; technology and technique focus on producing goods and offering services.

Generally speaking, you will combine the necessary requirements to perform a combination of all three tasks, starting with the creativity that you apply to your research, which you will primarily find in a technique when you look for a great idea. You will use technology, by virtue of the fact that you will develop a path for the transformation and creativity of that technique, and thus create potential for turning it into a scientific activity.

Similarly, in this chapter, you will be able to discover uses by combining procedures, which you can apply to the production of tools or techniques that can contribute to the innovation of a product, service, or result that you obtain with your observational and investigative approach.

Figure 3.3

The Technologist

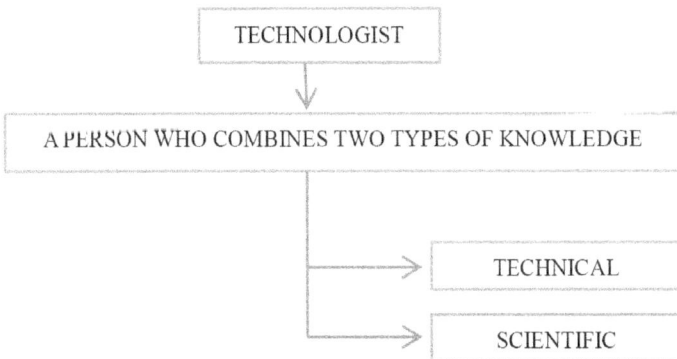

59

Researching an Idea

Researching an idea involves a process in which you use scientific methodology to obtain the relevant information to understand and apply knowledge. In brief, to research is to see in reality what others have not seen. We will use technical-scientific investigative tools as a fundamental and essential base for making a wide search for data related to your idea, with which we will be able to make use of these aspects.

1. Reality.

2. Analysis.

3. Formulation of a hypothesis.

4. Diagram for organizing data resulting from the research.

Every investigation generates procedures, provides results, and must draw conclusions. Besides, technical-scientific research stems from a real concept, researches it, analyzes it, formulates a hypothesis, and substantiates theoretical evidence.

Characteristics of Research

Research is a process of collecting knowledge and data from primary sources and processing them to create new knowledge. The essential premise of an investigation is the discovery of general principles. You begin by researching previous results, previous plans, and previous answers related to the specific product, service, and/or results of the idea you are considering. To do that you will do the following.

• Devise a methodology.

• Analyze the resulting data.

When you develop an innovative idea, you will design a detailed, technical, and scientific research plan, following specific procedures to discover several paths for the improvement of the clear representation. As a result, you will be able to remove barriers and find new variables or perspectives that contribute to the promotion of a different notion for your product, result, or service that you are developing.

Generally, innovation will be approached from various investigative angles. Three are listed here.

• Historic, what it was.

• Descriptive, what it is.

• Experimental, what it will be; all of this from the results that you will obtain from an innovative idea.

In Figure 3.4, you will be able to observe an outline of the most representative combinations, of the type of investigative framework that you will follow, and the variables that you will be able to refer to for feedback.

Description of How to Do Research on the History of an Innovation

In this type of investigation, you will be looking at an entire experience in any existing field that relates to the type of discipline that you are exploring. You will examine the technical-scientific aspect of your idea or any other aspect that shares or combines your specific talent with the way something was used in a clever or ingenious way in the past. That way you will find important data related to the most specific and essential functions that are characteristic and technical for your field of innovation.

You will search information in primary and secondary sources. This way you will explore it with internal and external appreciation, which will enable you to develop a historic overview of use and content. Also, you will be able to include an external investigative search of specific activities and characteristics, and be able to formulate a hypothesis and create a report on researching its history.

Descriptive Research

This type of investigation involves the search for records, data, analysis, and processes, as well as any current fundamental descriptive information. You will carry out a descriptive investigation by listing and describing the problem, formulating a hypothesis, searching for a theoretical framework, collecting data, and analyzing and interpreting the resulting information.

Experimental Research

This type of research encompasses the untested experimental phase, which explains the process or manner in which this product, service, or result originated. Therefore, in that investigation, you will observe a transformation or modification of information conducted in a controlled manner, looking at the origin of that exploration.

This type of research begins the process of establishing a cause-effect relationship to results that you set out to explore.

The outline of the description of the problem will consist of the following steps.

1. Formulation of a hypothesis.

2. Analysis of the research.

3. Experiment design.

4. Data verification.

5. Execution of the experiment and analysis of the results.

Figure 3.4

Model for Historic Research

Research concept for a product, service, and/or result that you wish to pursue.
- o   Compilation of information about the concept being researched.
        Primary Source
        Secondary Source

- o   Critical { Internal on the historic activity of content and use.

                  External on the historic activity of its use and form.

- o   Formulation of a hypothesis.
- o   Creation of a report on information about the historical background.

- o   Description of a problem.
- o   Formulation of a hypothesis.
- o   Theoretical framework.
- o   Collection of data.
- o   Analysis and interpretation.

MODEL FOR EXPERIMENTAL RESEARCH

- o   Presentation of a problem after verification of the bibliographical data.
- o   Identification of a hypothesis.
- o   Variables and analysis.
- o   Experimental design (ramifications or structure).
- o   Data applications and verifications.
- o   Execution of an experiment.
- o   Data information.

How to Organize Data after the Research

After you complete the investigation, the organizational outline of your inquiry can be laid out following the guidance of a technical-scientific document, shown in Figure 3.5. In this document, you will be able to illustrate the overall creative and descriptive development of the innovation process, with functional and practical characteristics involved in the transformation of a product, service, or result that you are working on, turning it into a final document.

This model is designed for and aimed at any person or group engaged in the development of innovative projects or concepts in any technical area, and at the post-research stage of a true creative idea for any assignment, presentation, initiatives, practices, disciplines, and professional and entrepreneurial practices of any specialty. The diagram is labeled technical-scientific, because it is the basic concept in innovation projects of any specialty or concept, inventiveness, or experience that you might have. In addition, it is linked to the term *scientific* because it uses a research method to discover something new, transforming it into a different concept.

This outline narrows the focus of all the concepts leading to a final report. The data relates to creativity, skills, and techniques produced to create a final document that facilitates the descriptive process and develops a research diagram of the innovation process for the discovery of a new product, subproduct, outline of new distribution channels, and ingenuity.

All this is included in a diagram or model for opening new businesses, helping with a school project with innovative characteristics, and presentation of an invention in the process of the development of a product. This model is to be used as a guide, in which to find support for the execution and development of a new product using some technical creative knowledge. That way you will simplify technology management, applicable to science.

You will use it exclusively as a basis for searching throughout to find a unique idea that you might discover and wish to carry out as a project using innovative skills and abilities. This outline will guide you to find results through a historic data collection process, and future update and research, which will produce a solid foundation for the presentation of your investigative phase.

Furthermore, this model diagram includes the three main elements of every universal research prototype, which are concept, problem, and methodology. You will always use it as a general guideline in the development of an idea, even though some of the components might not apply to the concept that you will be presenting. For example, if you are not formulating a hypothesis, you do not need to include it in your research plan. In addition, this will simplify the job of reviewers when it is time for them to evaluate the final document that you produce.

This model is complete and will help you achieve excellent results that you should be able to apply to a variety of fields where you can easily use it to innovate. This model also outlines processes that represent different variations of the components of the idea's significance and opportunities, objectives, scope of the concept, methodology, budget, equipment, and references, among others. By following these steps, you will be able to complete a final document.

The following illustration is a final technical-scientific document to carry out the research of an innovative idea, describing the components of every single step. This diagram is a guideline that you can follow for the analysis of any representation you are working on.

Figure 3.5

Model of the Final Technical-Scientific Document That Outlines the Research of an Innovative Idea:
Steps to Follow during the Process to Create the Final Document

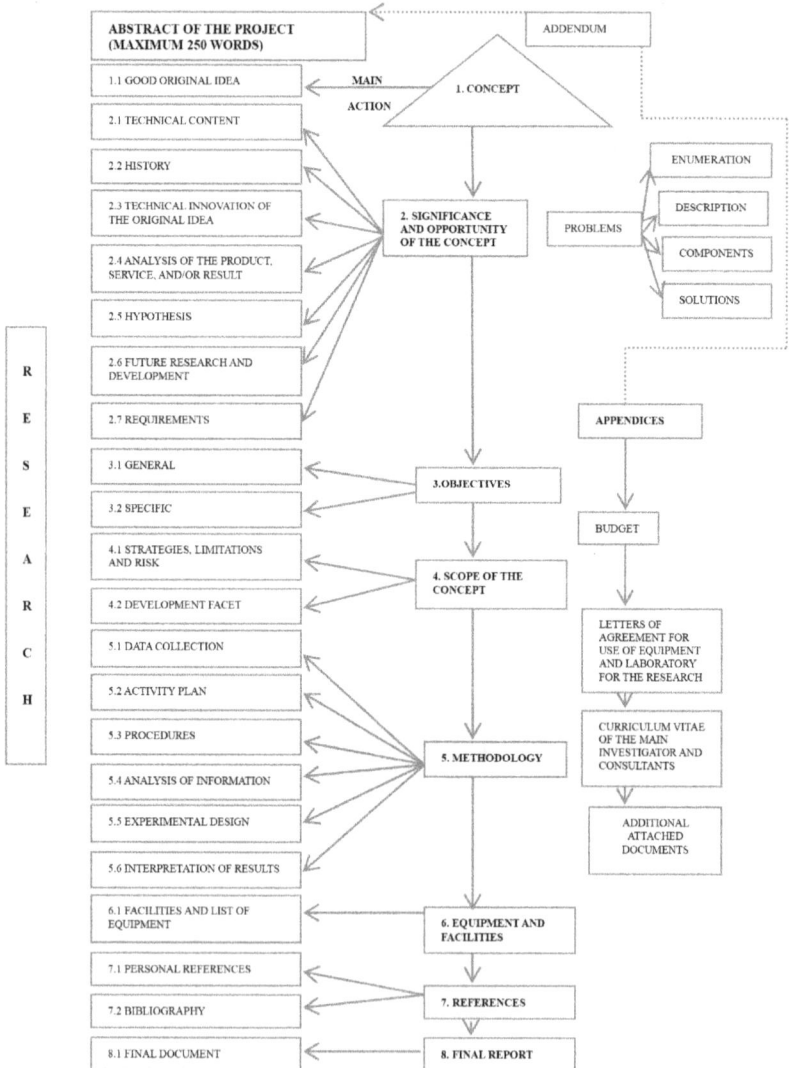

Described below are the components for an idea's technical-scientific research and guidelines for the completion of a final document.

Abstract

This is the first presentation page in a technical-scientific project where you will lay out a general summary of the project. It should be concise, a maximum of 250 words. You will begin with the title of the project and the name of the principal investigator, followed immediately by the summary. Then, you will layout the specific description of the activity that you are developing. This summary should focus mainly on the following three topics.

1. Objective of the project, activity, and its execution.

2. Relevance of the project for the program.

3. Scope and limits that you expect to reach with its main characteristics.

The description should be brief, concise, organized, descriptive, and well specified.

1. Concept

This term represents the first step of the process of creating a document or the title for the activity you undertake. It is where you outline the result of the investigation conducted in a specific area during the transformation of a technical-scientific innovation. It is here where you name the project, making a reference to the domain or type of work in an area of specialty.

Also, you should dynamically present any important information that you obtain, generating a specific result that you should lay out with technical and scientific skill during the conversion phase of the product, subproduct, new business model, new use for existing products, new markets for those products, new distribution channels, or simply an assignment about innovation for a school project.

You will call that representation the main action, because it is going to signal the point of departure in the development process toward a true idea or simply in the subject of interest with a transformative outcome.

1.1 Good Original Idea

This section is interrelated with your concept, where you will register an authentically good idea that you encapsulate in the formation of an action; you have developed it during the previous chapter, indicating the global aspects or content to be defined. You can include one or more complete good original ideas, mentioning the products, services, or results that you expect to obtain. This way you will begin the expanded approach toward the development of your innovation. With those ideas you will begin the path to an investigation focused on the area of innovation that you wish to work on.

2. Significance and Opportunities of the Concept

This is an extensive area to be documented, where you concisely express a series of descriptions, analyses, and the discoveries related to your innovation. In addition, you specify the value of carrying out such transformations and what makes the product, service, or result that you wish to undertake original. This process involves six important points that are required in the description of the documentation of an innovation project, included are technical content, history, technical innovations of the original idea, hypothesis, future research and development, and requirements. You will lay out these descriptions in a concise and descriptive manner in terms of your approach.

2.1 Technical Content

Here you will explain the technical-scientific importance, of that good original idea that you developed, from the economic point of view of the product, service, or result that you are pursuing in your desire to implement the innovation. This will be done as follows.

- Importance to the local, regional, and international economy.

- Impact on the creativity of the industry and contribution to employment.

- Competitive edge in the application of a technological innovation or any other type of use you might be able to present.

- Driving force of a specific result.

- Diversification of the result in its economic potential.

- Description of the dissatisfaction of the market toward an applied result.

- Preservation of and suitability for the environment during its development.

2.2 History

You should express the historic effects or profile of the product, service, or result that you intend to carry out in terms of its use, application, transformation, or similar previous elements, if present. Then, you will develop an overall evaluation of the result of that concept when you carry out the process of innovation for the first time. Also, during your research, you must make a note of any other type of application or use within the local, regional, or global context that you could develop or apply.

2.3 Technical Innovations of the Original Idea

Next you will describe how you intend to transfer the technological knowledge related to the specific product, service, or result that you undertake into an innovation. At the same time, you will describe its contribution, in terms of its potential, for the recipient of the project that you are preparing.

2.4 Product Analysis, Service, and Results

The purpose of this summary is to set the parameters of your research with preliminary data and results that you are going to develop in local, regional, and international areas. You should describe the essential basic functions and characteristics, developments, perspectives, and other extensions that you will develop and promote to bring about added value to your innovation, during the development process that you will carry out.

2.5 Hypothesis

You develop a hypothesis when you connect a theory and research that will lead you to new facts or discoveries. A hypothesis is a characterization that helps guide and outline an investigation, a definite direction in the search for a solution to a problem. The hypotheses are indicators of what you are searching for with the original idea. The essential characteristic of a hypothesis is that it always has to prove the related facts, that they are changeable, and that they establish a cause-effect relationship. In addition, the concepts should always be well defined during the development of the results that you are planning to implement with your innovation.

2.6 Future Research and Development

The research-and-development inquiry process is described concisely with a plan for growth that stimulates the future implementation of your project's idea. You will detail your research in perspective, with a vision of five to ten years, for the use and functionality of the product, service, or result that you are pursuing from the time of innovation, in addition, to expressing the functionality and value of the innovation. You should be able to compare similar products and their growth prospects at short and medium ranges and give examples of evidence of growth with data and results that you research or generate. Specifically, you will generate projection plans in a creative way in conjunction with the conclusion of an analysis of the product, service, or result that you plan to undertake.

2.7 Requirements

You should include every authorization related to starting and developing the project you are taking on, in your pursuit of specific results and your vision for establishing a business in a technical or research area. You must inquire about types of licenses, permits, laboratory authorizations, and research that you wish to conduct and all the necessary requirements for starting and developing that investigative phase. Also, if the project leads to a plan for a school assignment or innovation, you should obtain any authorization required for the development or execution of the project. You will be able to apply for licenses and permits during the research process. They will be helpful when you begin to expand on your research later and transition into marketing your idea.

Problems during the Development of the Significance and Opportunities of the Concept

If, during the description, you detect or observe problems in any of the boxes that slow you down, or you are unable to find a solution in your project, you should resolve them with research, energy, intelligence, and skill. In the context of research, problems give rise to solutions, which present themselves during the development of a project in any technical-scientific area, and represent a description of the significance and opportunity of the concept. The nature of these contextual problems can be divided into four categories, as follows.

Enumeration

This term refers to the process of enumerating, identifying, or specifying any enigma or unknown that presents itself during the development, definition, and exposure of the concept that you generate. In other words, what is the problem that hinders your process?

Description
You should indicate the most essential characteristics, mainly those that represent the origin of the product, service, or result that you obtain, focusing on its technological development and analysis that contributes to the identification of any problem that comes along with the opportunities and significance of the concept. You can use the Imagery Representation Model described in the first chapter to help you solve any problem that arises.

Components
Here you will describe all the factors involved in the problem that you uncover. That way you will create a perspective that will help you collect the correct documentation, conduct research, and include a better angle for analysis and observation of the composition of each element, helping you configure and solve the problem. You cannot solve a problem if you do not identify the elements of that problem.

Solutions
Once the important factors are described and understood, you can take the next step forward, which is to solve the problem. You will approach this exercise guided by your smart research and the originality of your imagination, creativity, and technique for describing the problem to arrive at a solution. You will have all the tools and will come up with all sorts of solutions if you describe each problem well, doing it in an orderly fashion, to uncover different approaches and finally a definitive solution.

3. Objectives
The execution of the objectives is the most important process in the elaboration of a project, which is why you should carry

it out with short-term and long-term priorities in mind, while keeping the scope and limits of the purpose or objective that you are pursuing within sight. You will envision these objectives as performing the functions of a real idea by using a process and in this way be able to achieve good results.

In the objectives phase, you will present your goal, the purpose and the reasoning for developing a good original idea into a process for achieving the goal. Your statement should be clear and precise. Every research project is assessed by the achievement of the objectives of the research being carried out, which is why the goal is an important element in the development of a project. There is only one question to be asked: Was the objective accomplished?

You will be able to show the progress and to measure the objectives during the project's development process, and they must be in accordance with your plan. This point is described in Chapter 5.

3.1 General Objectives

It consists of comprehensively formulating what you wish to learn or carry out. The comprehensive or universal approach requires presenting the outline of the development that you expect to implement in a general way. The statement establishes a specific action of the results that you obtain when you bring about the product, service, or result that you intend to research, and thus establish a goal for their achievement.

3.2 Specific Objectives

General objectives give rise to specific objectives. These objectives identify which actions need to be performed to develop them. Specific objectives are carried out in each one of the research stages, and they specify what needs to be done in a precise, well-defined, and individual way. In the end, the sum of the specific objectives will be equal to the overall objectives described in your project.

4. Scope of the Concept

This is the section of the research process where you indicate the importance of the achievements and the main purpose of a project's overall development. You will highlight the elements of scope and efficiency of the product, service, or results that are present in the transformative innovation process.

The description should be clear and include the maximum scope within the limits of the development of your innovation. Furthermore, it should present results that move forward and result in the implementation of the product or service and fulfill conditions or specifications of use, functionality, and effectiveness at their highest levels for the consumer.

In general, in the course of the research process, there is a high number of authors and researchers who neglect to define the scope of the limits of the original idea that they are developing, which is a reason for their failure. To refer to the limits of the scope in research means to determine the maximum reach and total use of that action and to set innovation specifications accordingly. During the technical innovation of a genuinely clever idea, those components that are described concisely by emphasizing the transformation process in detail could be adapted to the area where that innovation takes place.

During a technical development process, the work consists of defining the purpose and growth in the area of innovation. That area is developed in such way that can reach the maximum scope of the intended objective.

4.1 Strategies and Limits

It is here where the main skills are developed related to direction, technique, value, ability, and ingenuity of an innovative action that you wish to pursue to establish a business. That innovative action is characterized by setting up strategic points that set apart the product, service, or result that you are pursuing. This way you obtain a key characteristic that sets your product apart and makes it stand out from those of your competitors.

You should define specific characteristics to establish a viable and creative market competition, explaining the results that you expect to obtain and the inherent limitations of the idea being developed.

4.2 Development Facet

These will depend on the organization or agency where you seek funds or financial support. There will be guidelines with descriptions of the various phases for the presentation of your project.

Generally, there are four descriptive phases during the development process of an innovation.

Phase 0 is the presentation document, your active original idea.

Phase 1 is where you develop the first stage of the project, the experimental conversion phase of an innovation.

Phase 2 is for the study of the commercialization of the innovation.

Phase 3 is the execution process of a commercial business.

This design describes the significance of Phase 1, in which you conduct and synthesize the project that you are promoting and where you include summaries of evidence for Phase 2 (the study of commercialization), and the development of Phase 3 (your vision of an already established business).

5. Methodology

This signals the beginning of the method's description or working plan that you will carry out with specific procedures to foment your technique or the research of a true idea for the achievement of a described and systematic execution, with details in terms of how to carry out any innovation research that you present. It is done in an orderly fashion by listing the work procedures in detail. You will be able to add subgroup appendices based on your specific area of innovation.

That way you will follow an orderly and chronological pattern for the execution of all the components of how to implement that innovation properly. The following points are the areas of a working plan that you can follow during the methodology phase.

- Data collection.

- Plan of activities.

- General procedures.

- Information analysis.

- Experimental design.

- Interpretation of results.

You should be specific. Depending on the area of innovation involved, you will be able to follow the description of the titles appropriate for the methodology that you develop. Remember to carry out your methodology in order and in sequence; that way you will not forget any step included in your work plan.

5.1 Data Collection

This consists of the description and analysis of the process in the management of the data that results from the research of a good original idea. You will process every type of statistical information that contributes to the development and key application of the product, service, or result that you undertake. This way you will apply the key numbers or growth standards, quality, continuation, details, services, among other applications that you will be able to manipulate in the development of your work method. These data will become useful indicators in your development of analysis and direction.

5.2 Plan of Activities

Here you will proceed to itemize chronologically every activity or scheduled function that you carry out in your project. This will allow you to itemize your tasks orderly and not leave out any activity during the execution of your innovation. You must specify every task to be carried out, within the groups of actions and roles in a deliberate and orderly fashion.

You will be able to initiate your plan of activities from the moment you initiate your idea, keeping the process in perspective until you conclude the project. You can carry this out with the help of programs like Microsoft Project, Primavera, Genius Project, or simply by creating a table of activities where you list all the tasks to perform.

You should do this using a structured design that will help you properly project, control, and allows you to update the conclusion of the project. Figure 3.6 shows the plan of activities, with the different sections and their titles described. You will develop a plan of activities in accordance with the program and process of the overall function to perform.

These are the titles for your plan of activities: number of the activity, activity or function to perform, starting and ending dates, performance duration, specifications, and resources.

In Chapter 5, I describe more in depth how to plan a project, which you will be able to review later. Each of the points for the development of activities are listed here.

Plan of Activities

- **Number of the activity.** This is the sequential number of the activity or function that you plan to carry out.

- **Activity or function to perform.** This represents the description of the task or function to carry out.

- **Starting and ending dates.** This relates to the start and finish dates for the completion of the planned function.

- **Performance duration.** This is the duration or time allotted for an activity in days, months, or years.

- **Specifications.** This is where you can include the person in charge of a specific function or the person under that responsibility. Furthermore, you will be able to include any special characteristics of that specific function.

- **Resources.** You will specify, if needed, the type of financial resource that you will use in the development of an activity, or indicate the total portion of your project's budget designated for the activities related to that specific function.

Figure 3.6

Plan of Activities: List of Titles in a Plan of Activities

ACTIVITY NUMBER	ACTIVITY	STARTING DAY	FINAL DATE	DURATION	SPECIFICATIONS	RESOURCES

5.3 Procedures

This is the part where you apply the real methodology of the working plan of your innovation project, laid out in terms of the creation of a product, service, or result that you are planning to develop, with that creativity applied to different areas in accordance with your experience, function, and concept of the technical-scientific procedure. It is here where you express in detail your work methodology to implement the elaboration and transformation process for a specific result. You should use every applied technology in your process, from the initial phase to the completion of the result that you are pursuing.

5.4 Data Analysis

This is the action, process, and review of all the data and research of the study introduced in the methodology section of an innovation project. You will perform a data processing comparison and informative statistical research that can be used in any section during the development of the methodology or of another section in your project.

This way you will be able to review your procedure or work plan. With that data analysis, you will be able to expand the potential of the scope and restrictions of each key factor that you are testing, which you will use as a reference to successfully bring to fruition the important points of your project where you indicate growth, restrictions, records, comparative data, standard data, or any other factor or growth information.

5.5 Experimental Design

This refers to the schematic representation of your project's methodology or working plan, where you lay out in a sample model the working methodology that you wish to carry out in your innovation. This representation can be related to technology, crafts, or techniques in the fields of agriculture, ranching, medicine, biology, data science, or any other technical-scientific area that you seek to innovate and where you can apply your technique for executing a plan to develop your product, service, or result that you wish to undertake. You will produce a streamlined outline of your experimental search in the area of innovation that you plan to pursue, which will turn into a method with several samples showcasing your innovation prototypes.

During the design phase, you should produce four or five experimental samples. This way you will create a better representation of your transformational innovation and obtain convincing and more representative results. These results will help you answer your hypothesis, if applicable, and obtain decisive and demonstrable results. In addition, they will help you determine objectives, strategies, outreach, and limitations that you lay out for your project.

5.6 Interpretation of the Results

This step includes the answers that result from the analysis, research, and activation of your working plan, observation, and interpretation of all the data or the numbers obtained in the process of implementing the method and obtaining the results of that innovation. The information obtained will represent the results that emerge from your approach to the procedures. You can interpret those results with graphics or in writing, and then produce a document that will allow you to arrive at conclusions, including the history of your research guided by your work plan.

6. Equipment and Facilities

In this section, you will list the material, equipment, and infrastructure needed to transform a working method into an innovation using the results that you obtain from an original idea. In this area, you will indicate the facility where you will carry out your project, which can be a laboratory, an industrial setting with specialized equipment, an agricultural field, or simply your garage at home, where you will apply all the data to carry out the innovation with confidence.

6.1 Facilities and Equipment

This is the section where you will list the material, laboratory equipment, and all the necessary elements that you wish to use to help you develop your innovation. In addition, you will need to request letters of agreement that should outline or confirm an agreement or understanding for the use of the space, equipment, and the time to carry out your innovation. This letter of agreement will be included in the appendix (see the final document sample).

7. References

This section is divided into two representative areas that should include these items.

7.1 Personal References

Experts or consultants from your particular area of innovation that you could include in your project and who will advise you according to their skills, experience, and knowledge in the specific area of expertise.

You should include the most representative aspects of their experience for each one. You will determine in the work plan and in the planning of your project the stage where each one of your collaborators will participate and the type of activities they will perform.

7.2 Bibliography

Here you will list the references to books or sources, information, communication, or any other means used for research where the information supports the various phases of your innovation and where you describe the bibliographical data. The bibliography references used should be listed beginning with the author's last name, followed by the initials of the first and middle names. Then you will write the year the reference book was published, followed by the full title of the reference material or book, the volume number, if there is one, and finally the number of the page from which you extracted the reference or information.

In addition, you could list information for in-person communication or internet searches for any information that you have used in the study of the project.

8. Final Report

This will be the result of completing the full circle, where you craft a planned manuscript labeled final document, which is created with the sole purpose of developing and completing an innovation project. It should begin with the visualization of a concept or creative, ingenious, and conceptual notion that you carry out with a single goal in mind, which is transforming an idea whose exclusivity you will be able to register and patent. This way you will be in a position to carry out an accepted concept successfully when you create and complete a final document.

You will be able to participate in any competition for innovation opportunities in your areas of interest and to have access to any financial assistance that facilitates the start of your project and open the road for a business, research, technical concept, or simply for a school assignment.

This document should have no more than sixteen pages; separately, you include documents in the appendix, which are presented in the model for a final document.

Appendix

Individual documents should be included separately in the complete packet of the project and subject of interest, broken down into different areas. This packet of appendix documents consists of four sections.

1. Budget.

2. Letters of agreement.

3. Résumés of chief researcher and consultants.

4. Additional documents.

1. Budget

The budget will be divided into several sections, which will help better control each expense that you generate during the development of your project:

Personal Section or Section A

This will include all the participants (technicians, consultants, researchers, data processing personnel, students, and other staff) who collaborate in the development of your project. It will list hours of participation, benefits (if applicable), and each person's salary. At the end, calculate and enter the total expenses from Section A.

Equipment Section or Section B

This will include all the laboratory equipment, purchased or leased, needed to develop the project. You will include a list of all the equipment with its descriptions and prices, specifying each piece that you will be using, making notes on whether it is leased, contracted, etc. At the end you will tally the total cost for Section B.

Travel Section or Section C

You should describe all planned travel, domestic or international, that will help you obtain or research any information or experience for the project. You will list a description and purpose of each trip. At the end, you will summarize the total expenses for Section C.

Training Section or Section D

Here you will list the training, cost, duration, participants, and travel needed for training, which will help you in the development of your innovation. You will tally the total cost for Section D.

Section of Other Direct Costs or Section E

In this section, you will write down any material, publications, or any other direct costs that you incur for the development of your innovation project.

Finally, in the budget sheet, you will create a table with the cost summary of each section and calculate the total of your descriptive budget.

2. **Letters of Agreement**

These are created for, and required by, any institution that collaborates with your project and gives you permission to use its facilities, whether it is laboratory equipment, agreement of technical consultancy, or any participation in your innovation project. This document should describe dates, nature of the consulting or services, use of laboratories and tools, among others. The purpose of this is for the agency providing the financial backing to understand that there is commitment on your part for the development of your experiment, and that you are associated with laboratories or institutions with the necessary equipment to carry out your innovation work.

3. **Résumés of Chief Researcher and Consultants**

You will develop the curriculum vitae with the most outstanding achievements of all the participants, including their education, employment, publications, participation in innovative projects, honors, memberships in technical or professional organizations, and other applicable information.

4. **Additional Documents**

   Included here will be other documents needed for backing up or supporting your innovation project. For example, an additional letter for the research of some type of fauna or flora that you might need for the development of your innovation experiment, which might require some type of special permit from authorities.

SECTION 4
PROJECT

The idea that sparks an innovation later becomes a project, which is used to develop a business plan for research or for the preparation of a college assignment. The project phase requires putting into motion the pursuit of a specific goal and developing, among others, the capability of providing a service, the development of new or ancillary products, product improvements, and new markets. All of this is achieved using methodology models that help implement a transformation.

The success of a project is measured in terms of whether the objectives that were previously laid out are accomplished, together with the related peripheral elements. In this chapter, you will find a description of the development cycle of a complete project that can be used as a model for innovation in a professional area. It consists of nine sections with its main related features that should be taken into consideration.

CHAPTER 4

INITIATING A PROJECT

The word *project* derives from the Latin *proiectus*, which means "to propel something forward." It also represents an idea that you might have for creating something. Furthermore, project can be defined as a group of elements in a structure designed to achieve specific objectives or projected results based on planned processes. These deliberate processes are transformed into a framework for innovation, becoming a process in progress that can be modified and creative values changed within the specific structure that you have set up.

Throughout human history and in the course of our civilizations, we observe a great variety of ideas and plans for the elaboration of projects and the need for their development and use, as well as the achievement of acceptable objectives, even where no deliberate technique existed. Every period was characterized by a particular technique for the creation of products.

- Random technique (Stone Age).

- Artisan technique (Middle Ages).

- Technician technique (Modern Age, our times).

The use of techniques for the management of projects began in the 1940s. By the 1970s, using a technique had become commonplace, and there was a considerable surge in multidisciplinary teams devoted to research and to carrying out technological and architectural works. This was the beginning of innovation through project development and its application in the areas of these innovations.

- Operational innovation.

- Product innovation.

- Strategy innovation.

- Management innovation.

Each of the elements of these projects contributes to important events in the process of innovation of a product, service, or result generated from an idea, which will be outlined in this book.

The Reason for a Project

A project is a model, which is used to develop a plan to create something. A project helps us and guides us through every action required to achieve a specific objective. A project assists us in describing every technical and administrative aspect of a specific subject, problem, or applied methodology, which will culminate in a final document. A project outlines the evolution of a business plan or a school assignment that is developed from a distinctly creative and innovative idea, which makes it easy for a financial officer, a banker, investor, entrepreneur, businessperson, professor, advisor, or anyone else to review.

What Can a Project Define?

- The ability to perform a service (the opening of a business and its function as support to production or distribution).

- The development and creation of new products and ancillary products within their innovative frameworks.

- The guidelines for the improvement of a product, market, distribution, or formalization of ideas into a well-drafted plan with the characteristics of a project.

- The outcome of research, which can be applied to a product, service, or result.

What Is the Success of an Innovation Project?

Because every project is temporary by nature, the success of this plan should be measured in terms of the completion of the objectives. Your imaginative program will bring to life the transformation or discovery of a product, service, or result that you decide to undertake. As a whole and within the limits of your scope, together with the activity planning, budget, resources, quality, and foreseeable risks, you will illustrate in large part the success of a project and secure its approval by a project administrator.

That is, to ensure maximum benefits from a project, it is important to embark in a thorough analysis of the time allotted for all the scheduled activities planned before starting the project. A project should always begin and end in accordance with the projected plans for the activity, which, along with the budget, play a major role in the evolution of the activity in a scheduled, orderly manner.

Life Cycle of a Project

The life of an innovation project is comprised of several stages, which begins with the first phase or the initiation of the project, and sequentially progresses to the last phase, or the completion of the project. All the phases of a project are generally sequential, and their specifications are determined by the project administrator or manager.

Each phase can be self-contained in terms of its function: partial goals, type of product, scope of the research, results or ability to carry out a service whose development or delivery is required during a process. The life cycle of a project provides a time frame that makes it easier to manage and to provide flexibility in any area of the project that needs to be developed. Figure 4.1 is a diagram of the life cycle of any project, which includes the following elements.

- Birth of the concept.

- Organizational development and its preparation.

- Development of the project.

- Conclusion and completion of the project.

Projects vary in scope and complexity. Every project should follow a life cycle that aligns with a functional structure, so it progresses along the lines of that plan.

This structure is the starting point of all the stages of a project cycle. It will be useful in any professional field for planning innovation projects that you set out to implement. Additionally, you will have a better understanding of the importance of the roles played by each of the activities that you will need to complete while working on each phase of the project. This way you will have a good overview of the costs and materials needed to complete it. A project should always begin and end on time and on budget, having fulfilled all the planned stages.

The structure of the life cycle of a project is set in motion by the project leader or administrator, who can direct the different stages of the implementation of the project when it is time to innovate. Never confuse the life cycle of a project with the process of managing the project, because this function consists of many different tasks that are carried out in each phase of the project. The life cycle of a project is independent from the life cycle of the product, service, or result that you are developing.

Figure 4.1

Diagram of the Characteristics of the Life Cycle of a Project

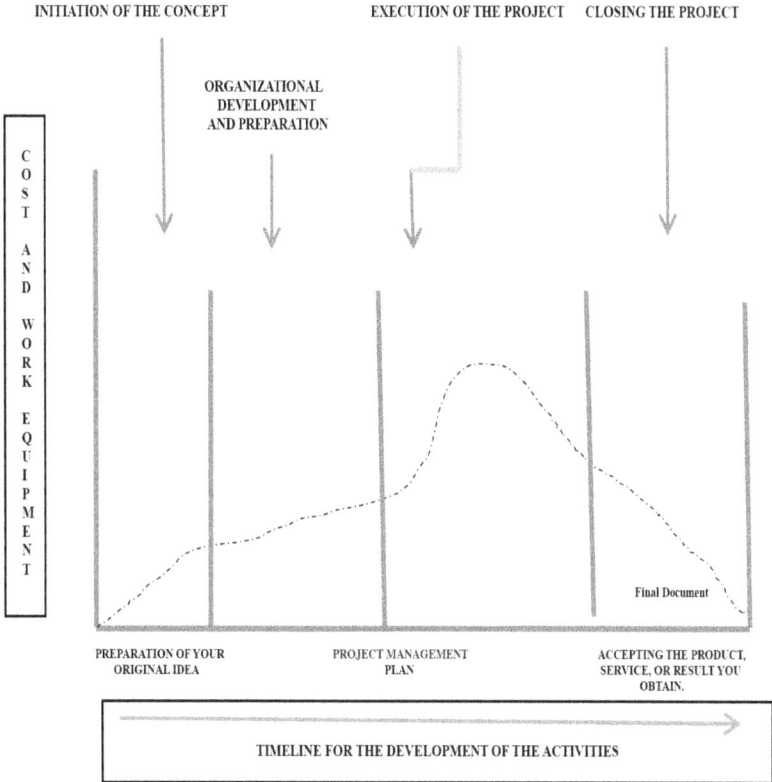

INITIATION OF THE CONCEPT   EXECUTION OF THE PROJECT   CLOSING THE PROJECT

ORGANIZATIONAL
DEVELOPMENT
AND PREPARATION

C
O
S
T

A
N
D

W
O
R
K

E
Q
U
I
P
M
E
N
T

Final Document

PREPARATION OF YOUR   PROJECT MANAGEMENT   ACCEPTING THE PRODUCT,
ORIGINAL IDEA   PLAN   SERVICE, OR RESULT YOU
                                                          OBTAIN.

TIMELINE FOR THE DEVELOPMENT OF THE ACTIVITIES

Type of Model for an Innovation Project in a Professional Field

Figure 4.2 shows a diagram for the process of an innovation project in a professional field. The diagram provides an outline of how to carry out projects with professional skills by following your document, which will consist of no more than sixteen pages. Not included in this document would be the attached pages or appendices, such as the curriculum vitae of the researchers, budgets, letters of agreement, and other additional documents that will be described later.

This diagram of the process includes effective guidelines for the realization of innovation projects in professional fields. It includes nine sections along with their main components, which will help you easily reshape and compose the final document. By doing this, you will complete a circle in the development plan or process to make the product, service, or result that you wish to innovate stand out and thus be able to compete for different programs that fund innovative ideas.

The goal of these programs is to promote and contribute to the creation and transformation of businesses with an entrepreneurial spirit through financial programs and subsidies for innovation, such as start-up centers, global associations, innovation-oriented business departments in universities, business incubator programs, microfranchise programs, foundations for business innovation, entrepreneurial financial programs, global venture programs, private foundations, angel investors, philanthropy groups, innovation development ventures, technology innovation programs, venture capital, scholarship systems, banks with investment funds for innovation, small business innovation research programs, mixed funds, and funding for women-owned or minority-owned businesses, among others.

Below is a description of all the components of the diagram for the realization of an innovation project for professional fields, with the main elements and functions.

Figure 4.2

Diagram for the Development of an Innovation Project in a Professional Field

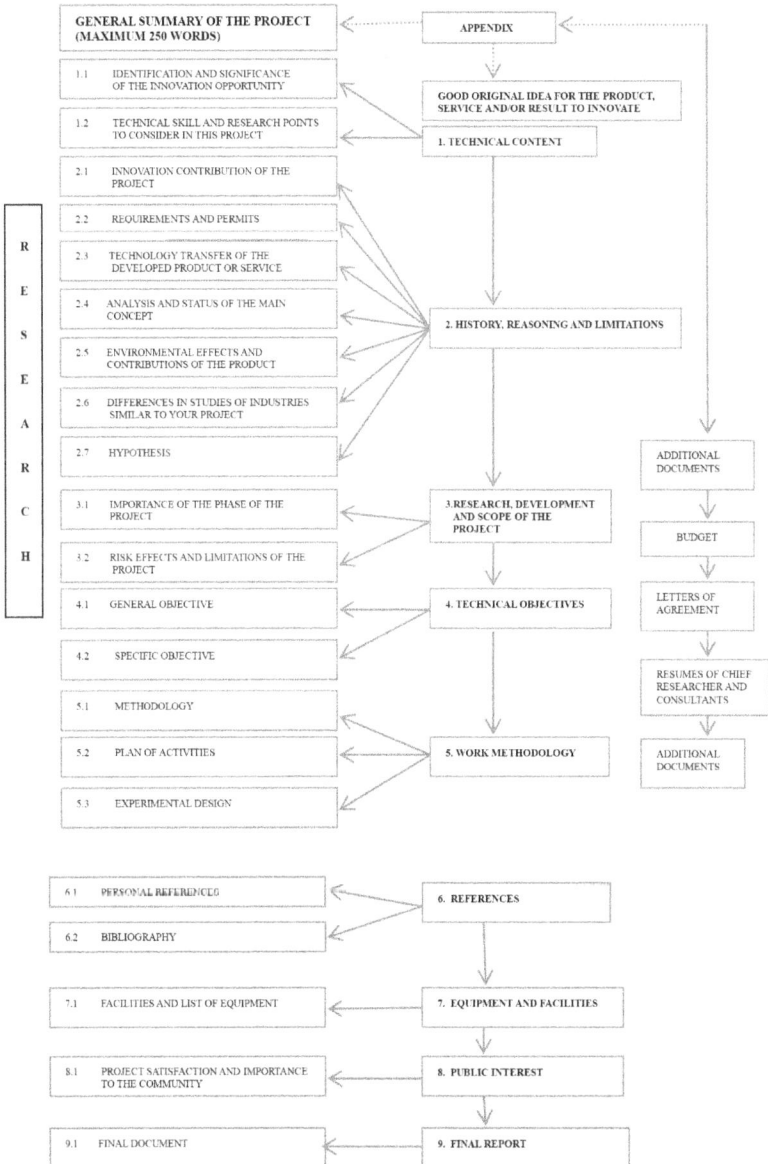

Summary

The first introduction sheet of a technical-scientific project is the summary of the project, with a maximum of 250 words.

Start with the title of the project and the name of the principal researcher; then write Summary. Next, you should lay out a detailed description of the activity that you plan to undertake. This summary is mainly concerned with the following.

1. Objectives of the project, activities, and their execution.

2. Relevance of the project to the program.

3. Scope and reach that you expect to accomplish with its main characteristics.

Your description should be brief, concise, well-organized, descriptive, and well-specified.

1. **Technical Content**
   This is the first section when you begin writing up a project, where you describe and provide a perspective of the project, stemming from your clever original idea that you are going to develop to innovate. You will begin the explanation process by identifying two components: (1) the opportunity of the product, service, or result that you are setting out to develop, and (2) its significance, along with the pertinent skills required for the innovation process.

   Your description should be presented in terms of the impact of your results to the economic sector at the regional, national, and international levels. Here you will highlight the economic potential and the diverseness of the product as the main focus. You should provide a brief summary of the market, comparing the production costs of your project to similar products or any other differences that you identify.

Remember that your product is original and ingenious in terms of its innovative value. You will concisely explain the favorable adaptation of the new technology that you are applying in your innovation, as well as the viability of your idea for transformation during the innovation development process of your product.

Details of the two components are described as follows.

1.1 Identification and Significance of the Innovation Opportunity
This point examines the concept of your idea and the opportunity that its application to an innovation project could present at a regional, national, or international level. You will explain, simply and concisely, the technical and financial potential of carrying out your idea, emphasizing the following growth points.

• Development of new technology.

• Combination of elements during the technology transfer and the viability that exists in the area or region for carrying out that project.

• Explanation for the reason why no other similar project exists or has been developed at the local, regional, or international level.

• Identification of the technical risks associated with this project.

    Also, you will mention the type of research that you are going to perform by describing a similar study carried out for that particular product, ancillary product, service, or result that you set out to develop, and the differences with your project.

1.2 Technical Skill and Research Points to Consider in This Project
You will describe the technology transfer and the technical ability presented in your innovation briefly and

descriptively. Also, you will list the main characteristics of the development methods that you will use during your innovation process, mentioning the technological and growth opportunities that your innovation will contribute during the most productive time.

2. History, Reasoning, and Limitations

This second section of the descriptive part of the initiation of a project is where you explain the main characteristics of your innovation together with vital information about the development, technology, contribution, production, requirements, analysis of the concept, implications for the environment, and the relationship of your idea's results to those of similar products. The components of this section are described as follows.

2.1 Innovation Contribution of the Project

This is the section where you outline your innovation's contribution to a product, service, or result. This input should include an explanation of the benefits of the innovation project for your local, regional, or international area, in terms of economic growth or project diversification. The number of innovative ideas that you can tap into is vast and diverse, so you can produce any idea that can be applied to a variety of disciplines and create a project for a business, for research, or for a school assignment about innovation.

2.2 Requirements and Permits

Some innovation projects require permits from local, regional, national, or international agencies, therefore, in this section, you will list all the permits and requirements needed to carry out your innovation project. First, you should list all the requirements for implementing this project, describing the organization issuing the permit, specific type of recommendation, and documents needed to initiate this project. You will be able to include a copy of the required permit or authorization in the appendix, in the section of additional documents. In addition, all permits and authorizations should be considered in your planning process, to help you schedule your activities in accordance with the times and permits required, so you can make them coincide and be able to continue with your innovation project uninterrupted. The process for planning a project is explained in Chapter 5, Planning a Project.

2.3 Technology Transfer of Your Product or Service
In this section, you will describe the technical and technological skills required to carry out the implementation of your product or service, by experimenting with innovative ideas and applying those ideas to the production process to achieve transformative results. You will examine the technological descriptive aspect of how to bring the product to fruition in stages or phases, which will make it easier to implement the creative process in any professional field by following detailed guidelines.

2.4 Analysis and Status of the Main Concept
In this section, you will lay out in general terms your research of the main areas and processes for the growth of your product, service, or result. You will also publicize the results of your developments whenever there is an opportunity, to make the innovation operations and transformation known. In addition, you will append to this section the reason for conducting this project, your commitment, and the prospects or probability for the innovation's success, as it relates to the highest quality of transfer.

2.5 Impact or Contribution of the Project to the Environment
In this section, you will indicate the connection of your innovation experiment to the environment at a specific

phase of its development process. You could mention general aspects of the main characteristics that result from the function, participation, or contribution of your product, service, or result to the environment. These functional aspects could include interactions with the air, water, animal life, or vegetation at the innovation stage. In addition, you will be able to include aspects of that correlation and their involvement in the environment. You will include this segment only if it applies to your innovation.

2.6 Differences in the Studies of Similar Industries and Your Project

In this section, you will bring up projects or industries that are related to the objectives of your experimentation process. You should describe the main characteristics and differences of the industry or projects related to your proposal or work plan, in other words, what your competitors have done and what you plan to do. You will detail projects completed in your regional, national, or international area, listing differences in the objectives, reach, and results achieved by your competitors. You will also be able to present a series of main production data from previous years and compare or highlight the results that you expect to generate.

2.7 Hypothesis

Hypotheses are indicators of what we are looking for in the context of a true idea. You develop a hypothesis when you connect a theory to research in a way that will lead you to the discovery of new facts or findings. A hypothesis helps you define a track and boundaries for research, which generates a new definite direction in the search of a solution to a problem. The main characteristic of a hypothesis is that resulting facts, which are variable and establish a cause-effect relationship, will always have to be proven. Besides, concepts should be well defined at all times during the pursuit of an innovation result.

3. Research, Development, and Scope of the Project

Section three or the implementation phase is where you lay out the research applied in conjunction with the development of techniques that are used when innovating, that is, you will write down the key factors in the development of your innovation. In addition, you will briefly describe the potential of your innovation to enhance or expand the product, service, or result that you set out to accomplish during the development of a project in a professional area.

3.1 Importance of the Phase of the Project
This is the section in which you indicate the significant value of your plan for achieving the intended results. That value is described in terms of its importance, relevant to the tools that you apply during the experimental phase and the best, expected results that you generate from that innovation. You will be able to transfer those expectations to the next phase of the project, for example, to carry out a marketing study of your innovation, or a survey for the opening of a business, among others.

3.2 Risk Effect and Limitations of the Project
Here is where you specify the consequences and limitations of your project in terms of its growth and direction, describing the following elements.

- Use of strategies in various stages of growth in the course of the innovation of the intended product, service, or result.

- Capacity and interpretation of the results in compliance with the direction of the project in terms of productivity.

- Effectiveness, quality, or any other distinctive feature that characterizes the product, service, or result versus those of your competitors in a genuine and innovative market.

- The effect and limits represent conditions whose single function is to measure the innovation techniques that you apply versus the results that you generate.

4. Technical Objectives

In the section on objectives, you set forth the goal, purpose, and objectives for the development of your original idea to achieve your goal, which is, to describe your innovation in a final document. The reason for carrying out your research should be explained clearly and precisely. Every project is evaluated in terms of the achievement of the investigation's goals, which is why the objectives are an important segment in the development of every project. There is only one way of categorizing it: Was the objective achieved? You should be able to relate the progress and to measure the objectives in the course of the development of the project, and it should go hand in hand with your plan, which is described in the Chapter 5. The objectives are divided into general objectives and specific objectives.

4.1 General Objectives

General objectives describe what you hope to know or achieve in a global or universal sense, which means generating a general statement of the development that you wish to accomplish. The statement will establish a general objective for the developed product, service, or result that you plan to research, and thus help establish a goal for its development.

4.2 Specific Objectives

Specific objectives stem from a general objective and identify the actions needed to begin developing them. Specific objectives form part of each of the stages of an investigation. The outline for these stems from what you want to accomplish, described in a specific, well-defined, and precise way. The sum of the specific objectives is equal to the general objectives described in your project.

5. Work Methodology

This is the section where you define your work methodology and you describe its structure, for example, an experimental innovation design for a professional field. This description is carried out in order of the procedures required, outlining the type of action for each one of the activities that you need to complete or accomplish to follow the methodology or system for the creation of a product, service, or result generated from your experiment. In this section, you will establish three important steps to complete this process.

- Method.

- Activity planning.

- Experimental design.

5.1 Method

This is the section where you describe your working process for the innovation project that you are planning. You will lay out this description in precise order with the number of activities, actions, personal and technical operations, and techniques that you will use in the development of your work method. This way you will verify your procedures and studies for the development process in their proper order. You can establish secondary notes depending on the approach you are using. In addition, you can include critical moments and periods in your experiment, along with key activities in the development of your innovation.

5.2 Activity Planning

This segment includes all the functions or activities of your plan in chronological order, properly organized and integrated. Schedule each task that you intend to carry out. You will begin your planning with a consecutive number of the function, followed by the starting and ending dates, and the duration of that activity in days, weeks, months, or years, followed by the names of the people responsible for that activity, or by any other information that you wish to include.

Finally, you will indicate the resources, which are the financial benefits or costs associated with those activities. You could use a software program like Microsoft Project, Primavera, or Genius Project to help you with this plan. These programs are designed well and have models for planning and illustrating activities using graphics. If you do not have access to these programs, you should be able to create an organizational chart using those headings, shown in Figure 4.3, to begin planning your activities.

In Chapter 5, Planning a Project, you will find the process for developing a plan explained in detail.

Figure 4.3

Activity Planning: List of Headings for an Activity Planning Chart

Activity Number	Activity	Starting Date	Ending Date	Specifications	Resources

5.3 Experimental Design

This is the step where you create a diagram of the work methodology for the experiment that you decide to carry out. The representative diagram will include a series of samples, data, and actions that lay out the steps to follow for the innovation process to produce the desired results. It is a good idea to include four or five samples to obtain a larger random representation to help with the interpretation of the resulting data. By doing so, you will have a more accurate and reliable sample representation of the innovation that you are pursuing. Also, in this step you will be able to interpret formulas, conversions, resources, and other key specifications of the experiment. The idea for the development of an experimental design is to observe the structural dynamic of the various components of the idea where you represent the transformation and configuration of the process.

6. References

This is the sixth descriptive section in the innovation process. References are divided into two distinctive sections, active and productive: the research and the assistance of the participants or contributing team with experience in the development and execution of your project.

6.1 Personal References

This is the section where you briefly describe the most important professional experience, participation, and contributions of knowledge of all the collaborators involved in your project, from experts, advisers, consultants, and personal communication personnel, including the principal investigator. You should list the professional, technical, or any other type of involvement in the project. Also, you will include the activities and responsibilities when you create the activity planning, describing the title, specific responsibilities, time, and the role they will play.

6.2 Bibliography

Every research project requires consulting bibliographic references. This section is where you include the references or information that you consulted and that you employed in your research, process, and execution of your project for the innovation of a product, service, or result that you plan to implement based on the original idea that you are developing. You will list the last names of the authors cited, in alphabetical order, followed by the initials of the first and middle names, and the year of publication, using all four digits. This will be followed by the pertinent title or the reference to the information. Finally, you will write down the volume number, if there is one, followed by the page where you found the information.

7. Equipment and Facilities

The seventh section is where you will list the material and equipment needed to carry out your innovation project. This revolves mainly around the development of the work methodology or the execution of the project's experimental phase. In this section, you will include the facilities, laboratories, and infrastructure needed to carry out your innovation. In addition, you will schedule their availability in the activity planning section. It is in this planning section where you will write down the functions of the required equipment and material and when they need to be acquired.

7.1 List of Facilities and Equipment
This is the section where you list all the material, equipment, and infrastructure needed to carry out your innovation testing. The first question should include the place where that test or experimentation will be carried out. For example, you might consider a specialized laboratory at a university, a clean room that meets certain characteristics, an industrial facility equipped with specific machinery, an agricultural and livestock field, or even the garage in your house, provided you have access to certain tools. In your activity planning, remember to include the list with information regarding the equipment's description and delivery date, the testing period, usage phases, and their functions.

8. Public Interest

This is the section where you indicate the public's participation and relevance in the execution of the innovation experiment or project to achieve the desired results. Public participation is important, and you should seek it throughout the development of the various phases of your innovation process to make the importance of the results that you achieve known.

You could share the steps or important data in a presentation during the development process to show the main features of your innovation, without compromising any confidential information. This way you will be able to share and publicize a particular facet of your innovation that you consider important for people to be aware of or simply to trigger public interest in your project.

You could also use this phase to establish a presence in written and electronic media, with maximum efficiency to increase awareness about your innovation and make your product or service known.

8.1 Satisfaction and Importance of the Project to the Community

Here is where you describe the benefits of your innovation project for the community; where you physically begin your experiment; and where the product, service, or result that you generate will ultimately have an impact. You could use any of the stages of the production phase: savings on services, design of a new tool or device, new development method, among others. The purpose of this is to increase awareness of the impact of your innovation in the community, whose residents will be its final consumers.

9. **Final Report**

This is the last section in the description of an innovation project for a professional field, where together with the other sections you will complete the circle of your original idea, which grew from a vision that you had for a particular professional field. This way you will complete the final report and turn it into a final document, which is the culmination of the innovation or transformation of a product, service, or result that you undertake.

This final document could in turn become a registered patent, which will establish its exclusivity and the terms stating that reproduction of the product, service, or result that you obtain from your innovation process is not permitted. It will also become your basis for competing for financial packages or funds to carry out that experiment. This way you will become a creative agent of change in professional settings, which you can put to practice professionally or use for a school project about innovation.

This final document should consist of no more than sixteen pages.

You will include the additional documents separately, as shown in the model for the final document.

Additional Documents

These are documents that you should include separately from the final document. This packet of additional documents includes the following.

1. Budget.

2. Letters of agreement.

3. Résumés of chief researcher and consultants.

4. Additional documents.

1. Budget
Expenses that you incur during the development of your innovation should be divided into the following sections.

Personnel Section or Section A. This includes all the personnel (technicians, consultants, researchers, data processors, students, or any other type of personnel) who collaborates or participates in the development of your project. You will include the number of hours of involvement for each participant in the project, a brief description of their functions, benefits (if applicable), and their salary. At the end, you will tally up the salaries of all the personnel under Section A.

Equipment Section or Section B. In this section, you will include all the required laboratory material or equipment, either purchased or leased, that you will use in the development of the project. You will include a list of all the equipment with their descriptions, function, or phase of the project where you intend to use it, in addition to its price. You will make notes of whether you have secured a leasing contract or any other type of leasing agreement. At the end, you will tally the equipment expenses under Section B.

Travel Section or Section C. This is where you include all the planned travel, whether domestic or international, for research or to secure information that will help you in the development of your innovation project. You will include a description and the purpose for each one of them. At the end, you will tally up all the expenses and under Section C.

Entertainment Section or Section D. Here you will describe any entertainment expenses that you incur, with costs, duration, participants, travel, fees, and necessary details that contribute to the development of that innovation. The total expenses will be entered under Section D.

Other Direct Expenses Section or Section E. Here you will include any materials, publications, or any other necessary expenses incurred in the development of your innovation project. The total expenses will be entered under Section E.

Finally, you will enter the total expenses for each section and reflect the grand total for the budget.

2. **Letters of Agreement**
This section contains all the documents required by any collaborating institutions that authorize the use of their facilities, laboratories, equipment, technical advising personnel, or have any direct or indirect involvement in your innovation project. This document should include dates, nature of the advising or the services, use of laboratories, tools, usage expenses, borrowed equipment, leases, among others.

The purpose of this section is for the financial granting institution to see that there is commitment on your part to the development of your experiment and that you are associated with institutions or laboratories properly equipped with the implements that you need to develop your innovation project.

3. **Résumés of Chief Researcher and Consultants**
    Here you will include the curriculum vitae or résumé with the most outstanding aspects of each person participating in the project, beginning with their education, employment, publications, participation in innovative development projects, honors, technical and professional memberships, among others.

4. **Additional Documents**
    Here you will attach documents that will support your innovation project. An example of this would be a letter describing your research of a particular type of fauna or flora that you will need to carry out for the development of your innovation project and for which you might need a special permit. Any documents of this type should be included in this section.

This description of the components of the diagram for the development of an innovation project for a professional field concludes Chapter 4.

SECTION 5
PLANNING

Planning is the art of organizing, and it constitutes the foundation of every project. It includes the projections, functions, execution, and implementation of all the activities that will come into play in the actual process, and it will determine the deadlines as well.

Planning is especially important when it comes to developing a product, service, or result that is innovative. Good planning covers the specifics of the entire process in detail and helps you stay on track and organized, improving productivity and promoting the timely completion of all the components that go into a project.

CHAPTER 5

PLANNING A PROJECT

Knowing how to plan an innovation project is an art that requires organizational skills and good sense. Planning can be defined as the process of determining future actions. Generally speaking, the planning process consists of considering different alternatives for a course of action and deciding which one is the best.

Planning is the first step in the management of any project, in which problems are identified, past experiences analyzed, and plans and programs outlined. To plan is to go through the process of deciding which functions will need to be carried out in the future. Planning is essential in the development process of any project or idea, because it helps you foresee as many tasks as possible, in such a way that nothing is left out if the plan is well designed.

Planning is an important process in the execution of any innovation project. It always begins with an assessment of the future, which is a requirement for making the plan. This leads to an accurate prediction, which determines the real action that is used as a basis for mapping out a projection in writing. That is why being a project manager is one of the most difficult jobs in the world.

When your working plan for the development of an innovation project is completed, that is, during the first phase, it will include an experiment or the application of a technology transfer, as described in Chapter 4. This way the main objective of the project is established.

The next step is planning the activities that need to be implemented to carry the innovation project to fruition. Laid out simply in Figure 5.1 are the most important elements, which represent a unique and complete design layout, including deadlines. This is a determining factor in bringing an idea to conclusion when you follow the process.

Figure 5.1

Activity Planning Chart for Your Innovation Project

CONSECUTIVE NUMBER	MAIN ACTIVITY	DURATION IN DAYS	BEGINNING DATE	END DATE	GUIDE	RESOURCES	J	F	M	A	M	J	J	A	S	O	N	D

MAIN ACTIVITY	DATES	MEANS	TIMES

The activity plan for an innovation project is divided into four distinct areas, as follows:

1. Main activity.
2. Dates.
3. Means.
4. Times.

1. Main Activity

This is the first section reflected in the chart. You will include each activity that you are going to carry out, listed in order with consecutive numbers. This will be followed by the main activity, where you will write out sequentially the essential function or activity for each technical and scientific aspect of your project in a precise and objective manner.

2. Dates

In this section, you will include the total time needed to complete the work or activity for the main function. You will be able to lay out a plan for every function needed to implement your innovation project, from the beginning of the process to the last task. This period of time can be measured in days, months, or years, depending on the type of project that you develop, including an estimate of the time for each activity.

Generally, organizations or institutions that grant funds stipulate a specific time to complete the innovation project (about six to eight months, on average). If your project extends past the estimated time, you could request a letter of extension to finish the project, which should be attached to your activity plan or schedule.

After the time duration, you will find the starting date, where you will indicate when you plan to begin the main or required activity. Next, you will establish the ending date, where you will write down the end of the project or activity. You will establish these dates based on your information of the time required to carry out an activity from beginning to end. The established sequence should be followed closely, according to plan; if there are any unforeseen circumstances you should record them under the Means column. Remember that all the activities form part of your original plan and should be executed in order and with precision during the development of that innovation project.

3. **Means**
    This is the third section where you will include, in consecutive order, all the activities that are related to one another or have some correlation and can be performed and organized together. These are laid out sequentially and constitute what it is called the guide.

    Generally, means are used when the main functions depend on one another and work consecutively throughout the process from beginning to end. The main activity is going to rely on a guide, from the moment the process begins to the moment it ends. Each guide will focus on a particular activity and a series of specific dates that will signal the beginning of that activity.

    For example, when the main activity has started, and it encounters a guide that is at the halfway point of completion, you can indicate the starting and ending dates with numbers to reflect the progress you have made in the completion of that activity or function.

    The column in Figure 5.1 next to the guide is for resources. Here you will include a list of all the resources required for the main activity. For example, if it is a human resource and you need to hire an electrician and an electromechanical technician, you will write down one electrician and one electromechanical technician and assign a percentage (200 percent). This way you will establish the actual need for a human resource in numbers. You could include other aspects in this column according to your needs (other resources can be added based on the needs of the particular project).

4. Times

In this fourth section, you will illustrate graphically—with figures, bars, lines, arrows, or any other type of symbols—the amount of time required for the activities. For example, you could include icons for section two, or symbols for section three, to reflect the time or duration of the development period for each activity in your project, which could be measured in days, months, or years. In addition, you should graphically indicate the starting date for each function or activity in your plan and continue to the ending date.

In this section, you will also indicate any updates that you make to your guides or to its related activities so you can check the progress of every function, and the stage of the planning and development of your project. This way you will be able to see the progress, get feedback, and have an overview that will help you track and evaluate the overall stage of the development of your project.

This could also be a tool that your team members or any other person interested in becoming acquainted with your project could use to consult the plan and to monitor the progress of the activities and the required stages of development of this innovation project.

Generally, one or more of the following graphing charts can be used.

Graphing Charts

Bar Chart

Also known as the Gantt chart, a bar chart is most commonly used for simple projects. This type of chart shows all the information related to the activities vertically, and it shows the dates and duration of the activities horizontally, listed in correlation according to their starting and ending dates.

These graphs are a relatively easy way to help you visualize and manage the different steps of the project's planning and to see all the activities at a glance, which is the most significant function of a project plan.

Flowchart

This chart is similar to a bar chart. This type of graph only shows the beginning or the ending of the activities, the results or the ability to carry out and complete a service that is required within a process, phase, or project.

Network Diagram

This chart is a graphic representation of the relationships among all the activities of a project in logical sequence. These diagrams are created manually or with a project management program. This diagram includes bar and time scales that represent the duration of your activities, using a project's logical representation.

The Planning of the Technical-Scientific Document for Any Professional Field

In every prototype or model for a project document that is technical-scientific in nature or related to a professional field, there is a section in the plan of activities where you can include, in chronological order, your projection of the overall activities or functions required for the completion of the innovation that you are planning to carry out.

Chapter 5 refers specifically to planning a project and includes the most important elements for creating a plan. For an innovation project, your plan will include specific and relevant elements, because it is here where you develop and from where you manage all aspects of the implementation of the project. These basic elements represent landmarks that illustrate progress and that are valuable not only to the principal investigator or team but also to any person who is interested in becoming acquainted with this type of innovation.

These elements reflect the work methodology, specific functions of the activities, duration in terms of time, party or person responsible, monitoring, and the stage of development of the projected activity. In addition, it functions as a graphic representation of each planned activity.

This plan of activities will be one of the sixteen pages that you will need for the project's final document. You will be able to share the plan right when you begin to implement your innovation, as this document also works as a guideline for every person on your team tasked with carrying out the innovation.

Remember that planning is the art of organizing the activities and functions that need to be carried out. In other words, if you develop a well-thought-out and thorough plan, you will control not only your current plan but you will also have the framework for projects in any other area to which you decide to apply them. You will also build opportunities for potential new creative ideas and for proposals not only in your specific area of specialty, but also in any other areas within that innovation framework.

I conclude this chapter by citing the planning strategies of our ancestors, such as the Nahua, Aztecan, Mayan, Incan, Egyptian, and Roman civilizations, that laid out their plans for urban activities and operations, their agricultural and seasonal activities, and their future projections on calendars. Then, we will move on to Chapter 6, which refers to managing a project.

Figure 5.2 shows a planning chart from the Mayan civilization, where symbols represent writing and the interpretation of Mayan ideas and sound combinations. This type of planning was developed to predict future events or activities and their timing (*The World Book Encyclopedia*, M 13, pg. 325, 2016).

Figure 5.2

Planning Chart from Mayan Civilization

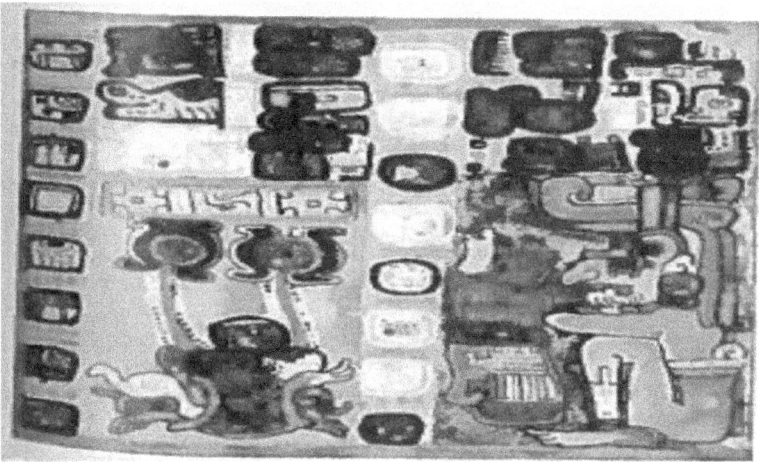

Example of a planning chart from Mayan civilization. In addition, this civilization produced books (made of fig leaves) to create astronomy charts, information about religious ceremonies, and calendars of agricultural, fishing, and hunting activities for subsistence. Worth mentioning are their planning charts representing eclipses and orbital descriptions of the planet Venus.

SECTION 6
MANAGEMENT

Management is a vital aspect of the innovation process. It begins at the moment you have the vision for a potential idea, and it continues with the application of all the specific principles at every stage of the process. Management provides the backbone needed to drive the idea through all the stages of a project and to transform the main concept into a blueprint for innovation that will be used to fulfill the four main management principles: strategy, resources, time, and budget.

Each one of these principles comes with a series of steps that give shape to the project and help move the activities forward. It is important to understand both the scope of the concept and of the project for each one of the elements that you implement in the development of your innovation plan.

CHAPTER 6

MANAGING A PROJECT

Every project is a design, which must include, in addition to the technical, scientific, and budgetary elements that are linked to their objectives, guidelines that help with the operational aspects of the management and control of the idea during the innovation process. In this chapter, I describe the key elements of the management principles to guide you in the development of an innovation process.

The management of a project begins at the moment you have a vision for a potential idea that you wish to pursue and that you are determined to creatively carry through to fruition, by implementing strategies that help you achieve the desired transformation. This transformation process will follow a path to action that will convert an inventive idea, skill, or ability into a real concept, which together with the necessary tools will help you carry it to its final stage with the goal of creating a new or ancillary product, service, or result by conforming to established goals and strategies.

The difference between goals and strategies is that goals are long-range actions that can be in the development process for years. Also, goals help strategies move forward in the same direction. Strategies are defined as the aggregate of systematic actions carried out during a defined period of time, in which they can be implemented to produce a specific goal or mission.

Goals and strategies will help you in the project development process and allow you to create a management protocol to follow to turn that plan into a final document. The type of management function will define and determine the decision-making process for each activity during the development and its projected function. Also, the management protocol for your innovation project should include the following elements: strategies, resources, time, and budget.

These elements will help you with the orderly transition between activities through the management phase to be able to carry the project to fruition in a concise, realistic, and streamlined manner and with optimal operational skills. During the strategic development phase, it is important to remember the following key elements, represented in Figure 6.1, which are inferred in the process of a management project.

1. Devising proper strategies to carry an innovation protocol to fruition.

2. Proceeding with and coordinating the management process activities that contribute to the innovation.

3. Transferring the product, service, or result that you obtain to an organized management plane in a creative manner with the available resources.

4. Remembering to always deliver the project on time according to the dates stipulated and create a detailed, updated, and exact budget for your equipment and material estimates with truthful figures, based on data from your research (see description for creating a budget in Chapters 3 and 4).

Figure 6.1

Elements for the Management of Strategies, Resources, Time, and Budget When You Apply Your Skills in the Management of an Innovation Project

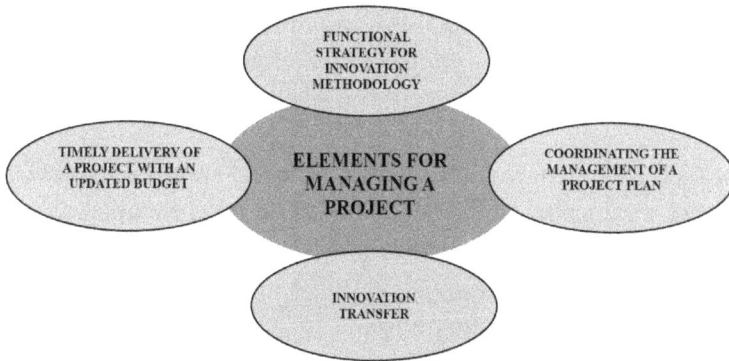

How Do the Intervening Factors Work in Practice in the Management of a Project?

The intervening factors in developing the management of an innovation project and their application contain certain basic key process elements that characterize the technical-scientific or professional area of your practice.

These four factors, properly coordinated during the development of a product, service, or result, identify a series of skills and the knowledge that you can apply when you are ready to innovate, which refers to the process of modifying or changing something to create a final product of transformational functional characteristics.

The framework of the two documents presented for the innovation models should always follow the order of the design process and the outline of the plan described, which are explained in Chapters 3 and 4, respectively. The only aspect that will change is the function of the specific innovation. This way the management process will be driven by the four factors that take part in the structure of the innovation project.

Your technical and professional skills for carrying out the functions and the work methodology, which is the process of implementing the practical and descriptive elements of an innovation, and are most important for a project reviewer or for any person interested in knowing how you are going to carry out the innovation, should be included in each of the technical-scientific documents.

The sections where these should be included are the scope of the concept, the professional section of research and development, and the scope of the project, because these are key areas for outlining strategic elements, risk awareness, and scope presentation, for the new idea as well as for the project.

Using a data system that properly interprets the basic points of the model will help anticipate potential solutions and allow those data points to become the benchmark or basic referents to be surpassed to obtain better results in your innovation experiment. For example, in the field of aviculture, a growth rate versus feed supply strategy would be described in the experimental design and work methodology sections of your innovation process plan. In this example, you would introduce strategies in the form of numbers, which would become your data bank models for those rates and which would be your threshold for obtaining the best results. In this case, the success of your projected strategy would be to improve the proportion of the feed rate to achieve the best outcomes.

For an example in a technical-scientific field, think of a commonly available measuring tool in which the units are expressed in millimeters. Your idea and your research identify the need for a tool with different basic attributes that is more accurate than the existing one. In your innovation, you will create a strategy with the specific characteristics that you wish to achieve, which you will carry out accordingly to produce a tool with the desired specifications to surpass the reference model.

These reference models are necessary and useful in your methodology phase, because they help you develop benchmark objectives to attain and surpass. This methodology will help you navigate the individual or collective coordination of activities during the management of a project to achieve the best product, service, or result.

Anything you do in the development process to create your product, service, or result should be included when you implement your methodology and experimental designs. Both processes should be performed with attention to detail to achieve the desired design results in a representative manner. You should also include the personnel in charge of each activity, which together with the available resources and time will carry the project to fruition.

You should complete your final document, with the delivery dates and the funds that you have applied for and that you will have available, in compliance with the requirements for the submission of a final document. In addition, you should create an updated budget of all the materials, equipment, and resources involved in the development of your innovation.

Strategic Processes of a Development: Their Function, Objectives, and Activities

In an innovation project, you should aim at applying five elements that will help you with the optimum management and completion of each objective, activity, and responsibility that support a series of administrative and operational tools, represented in Figure 6.2, which illustrates the strategic process for managing a process. Figure 6.2 symbolizes the connections within a strategy in its different stages, beginning with an overall specific objective for the process. They are as follows.

a. Formulation and development of a general and specific objective.
b. Strategy development.
c. Strategy evaluation.
d. Design of a systems organizational structure.
e. Strategy control.

Figure 6.2

Diagram of the Strategy Cycle for the Management Process

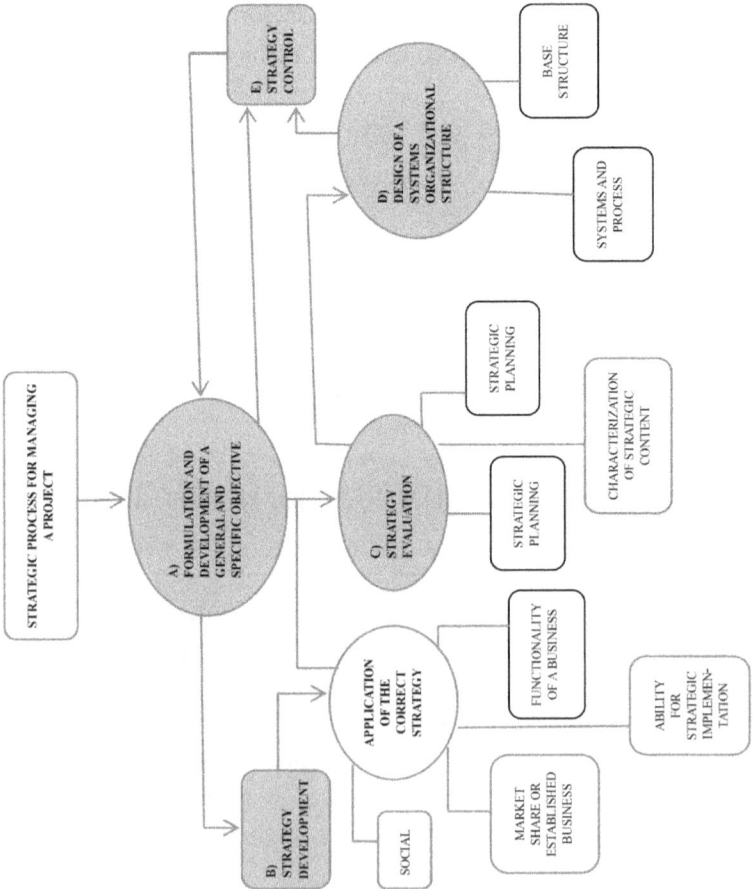

This diagram represents the different stages of a strategic process for an innovation. Each stage presents the main characteristics or basic elements that could be used, regardless of the area of innovation that you decide to pursue. It also indicates the specific sequential steps to follow, which you could apply according to the situation and how you decide to proceed with an organizational business or structure. You will also be able to establish boundaries or shortcuts for a strategy, moving from a functional skill that you present on to the evaluation, until you complete the entire strategy.

Each one of the components of these steps is described as follows.

A. Formulation and Development of a General and Specific Objective

The formulation of clear and concise objectives is described in the first step of the strategic process for managing a project. This process marks the beginning of the innovation's strategic actions, which should be implemented in the context of a plan, together with the objectives and goal of the project or of the organization. The goal and the objectives should be specific, measurable, attainable, real, and on schedule.

The formulation of objectives is a complex process, especially when it comes to innovation. Objectives are the most important elements in the development of a project, which is why you should always establish priorities based on three main guiding points.

1. The type of organization involved in the innovation (normally a business would have different objectives than a university, a hospital, or a nonprofit organization).

2. Strategies and activities to achieve the objectives should always be organized in order of priority.

3. The attainment of the objectives should be planned out realistically, be measurable and concise, and have a deadline for achieving results.

133

B. Strategy Development

The development of strategies refers to the processing of skills, which are the key to solving a series of activities while they are being formulated. At the beginning of the process of creating an innovation strategy, the process, the rational conclusions, and the adjustments, in other words, its formal context, will require four different strategic levels.

1. Social Strategy

This concept considers the skill factors where the entire organization involved in the innovation project has a role to play. The process defines the function of the complete social organization, where the social strategy of every person from the organization who is involved in the innovation process and who participates in any of the related financial objectives will be accounted for.

2. Corporate Strategy

This strategy level relates to any innovative business activity involved in the transformation, modification, creation, and ideation for carrying the idea to commercial fruition. This strategy demands conceptual guidelines, awareness, and balance to take the ideas from concept to reality. This step will help identify what percentages will be set aside for the innovations. It will also help define the skills required to maximize the attainment of the objectives.

3. Business Strategy

This component refers to the functional strategies of small and medium businesses. The strategies will identify how products behave to determine how the innovation process should be implemented to be competitive by following clear and concise objectives. This will also allow you to use integrative strategies in the different areas and activities to be able to maximize resources. This type of strategy requires observing how the product performs or functions in the industry or business context so you are able to gauge its competitiveness.

4. Strategy of Area Functionality
This process entails two types of strategies.

- Integration strategies of the various subfunctions of an activity.

- Strategies relating to a series of activities associated with policies of change that can occur in functional areas. This involves not only strategies for the effective management of inventory, production, planning, integration or automation, but any change in technology affecting the various areas that take part in the innovation as well. This way you will be able to control any changes in your innovation activities with simple technological modifications.

C. Strategy Evaluation

The evaluation of strategies is an analytical process that helps identify how future impacts on a particular skill or ability might affect the achievement of functions and activities in general. These can be more prevalent in areas of design and planning, implementation, and characterization of the main elements, which are as follows.

- First, how successful was the development of the first strategy?

- Second, how likely is it for that strategy to be developed in the future?

- Third, how effective will the analysis of the development of a series of alternate strategies be for executing an activity in the future?

You will need to evaluate the effectiveness of a proposed strategy on a continuous basis by doing the following.

- Reviewing the objective constantly to determine if the existing or proposed key elements respond to the needs of the proposed objective.

- Identifying a strategic planning method, in other words, establishing credibility parameters and analytical principles when you develop a strategy process.

- Evaluating the strategic content to determine if there are consistent check points or controls that have the capability of evaluating your strategy.

- Devising an implementation strategy in case there is an organization or business that can perform the existing or proposed strategies, which should derive from the projected resources listed in the plan of systems and processes that the organization can perform.

Once these evaluations have been put in place, you will be able to establish the best practices and to implement them. During the implementation process, do not forget to assess the strategies by considering the following points.

1. Establish a strategic plan that calculates percentages of variation in the success of the development within the resource plan of a business or organization. This should be determined by using the various strategies that contribute to the innovation of your product, service, or result.

2. There is a "no compensation" element in the implementation of a strategy and you should develop it by using control mechanisms, with a reliable alternative that does not consider the possibility of evaluating a potential

during the innovation process.

3. There will always be fissures or splits in the strategies, especially during the innovation implementation phase of any product or service. These fissures shorten objectivity, effectiveness, and timing parameters during their application. In addition, they negatively affect the success of a business or organization. If this happens, you should adopt a new strategy where there is greater functionality for the main activities driving the innovation.

The direct implementation of these three factors creates an effective tool for assessing and developing a project at long range and thus create a successful organization or business. That is why you identify the components separately in the strategic management process. On the other hand, you can divide the process or strategic models into parts. These steps are highly recommended and sometimes required in the development of one or more strategic components of the innovation's management contingency process.

D. Design of a Systems Organizational Structure

The design of a systems structure is the most important strategic aspect in the management of a business or organization where innovation in the value of the product, service, or any other type of innovative application is involved. This organizational structure should primarily contribute to modifications in its configuration, because it is at this stage that beneficial changes can take place by incorporating new strategies that affect its overall appearance in terms of design, systems, and processes to be transformed into a table of new skills, which include the following.

1. A basic structure with the planning, method of specialization, coordination of departments, actions to be delegated, and authorization.

2. Systems and processes play a role in the orderly management of an organizational structure to make it possible to carry out the innovation process successfully, integrating all the required components to fulfill that task, which will be used to develop the final document. This document is the culmination of the structure that completes the circle of innovation and that illustrates a project of a technical-scientific nature or of any other professional field, achieved by following a system and a process for the particular product, service, or result.

The management section, where ideas for the transformation are included, which will act as a guide, organization, and direction for an innovation project, should be developed with a creative and entrepreneurial spirit. You should also consider up-to-date information and knowledge to be able to achieve transformational results, whether for opening a business or for a school project about innovation, keeping in mind the following types of opportunities, which work synchronously.

- Functional opportunities.
- Market opening opportunities.

Functional opportunities are the opportunities presented by any business or industry that is staging a function or undergoing a change at a specific moment in time. They represent the unexplored areas of the market. These are the openings that might exist in businesses and industry, where there might be market opportunities for a product or a service that could be beneficial to consumers.

In the context of functional opportunities, the boundaries of a business or a particular industry are well defined and identified, and the rules of the game are well known. Companies try to surpass their rivals to gain a larger share of the existing market. As the market becomes saturated, the profitability and growth margins diminish, products become undifferentiated, and competition requires greater effort.

Opening opportunities are defined as the areas of the market that are untapped, where a novelty can create highly profitable demand and opportunities for your product, service, or result. Although some of the opening opportunities are on the fringes of an existing business or industry, most of them stem from functional opportunities, with the expansion of the boundaries of this type of industry.

With opening opportunities, competition becomes less cogent because in that particular instance, the rules of the game do not apply. With functional opportunities, it is always important to maintain a healthy competition for your product or service. You can gain an advantage in that competitive arena by delivering great quality, service, variety, and innovative value with skill and talent. Functional opportunities are important and will end up being widely accepted in the business world.

A business should always aim at surpassing its competitors to achieve new growth and profitability. Unfortunately, opening opportunities, for the most part, are not well defined. Strategic thinking focuses mainly on strategies for functional opportunities where competition is more prevalent.

E. Strategy Control

Strategy control is a process where the action of a specific strategy or ability acts as a link to the organizational structure of a business, and with the objective for any activity that has an absolute active control of the ingenuity and skill that you have devised with a verifiable and successful record. You will be able to simplify during the formulation process, go directly to an evaluation, and control a strategy directly. You will proceed according to the objectives that you implement and to the different branches of innovation that you undertake.

The purpose of this simplification is to observe how a strategy that you have devised works, how it outlines the plan and the content of the application, and the potential fissures that you might be able to detect to determine the progress of your strategy. You will carry out a verification of the skill to every objective and be able to produce a draft of the main sections of the final document that you plan to deliver with absolute confidence.

Resources, Time, and Budget

The concept of resources, in the context of the management of the process to create a new product, service, or result, encompasses an extensive, wide, and descriptive area that presents you with new opportunities in terms of time, investment, equipment, and budgets. In addition, all the information, one way or another, contributes directly and indirectly to the creation, application, and transfer of a project into a final document.

This section deals with the most important factors in the area of resources that play a role from the beginning of an innovation process, illustrated in Figure 6.3. You will be able to apply them to any area of innovation that you develop. These resources are divided into four main categories: financial, educational, human, and material.

Figure 6.3

Graphic of the Main Resources Employed during the Development of an Innovation Project

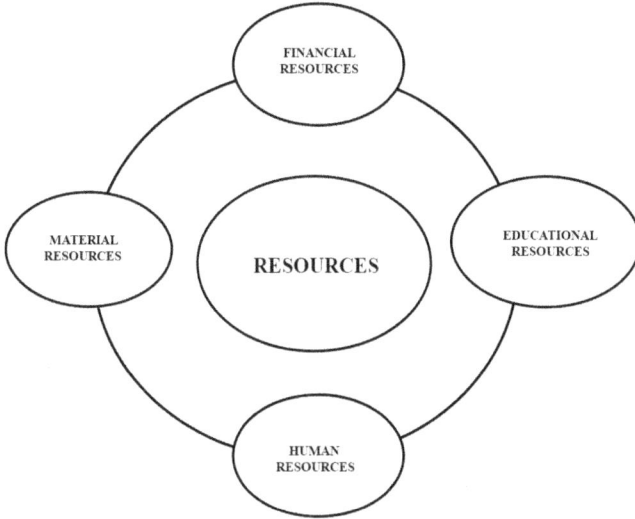

In the process of developing an innovation project, these are the main four resources, which are represented with the most basic and easy elements to be implemented. For that reason, they can guide you and assist you in the preparation, research, and involvement of these resources to help you carry your innovation project to fruition.

1. **Financial Resources**

    These resources include all the financial support that you have access to and apply for to embark on an innovation project's initial phase or growth process, which you can take full advantage of by using the tools provided in this book to help you obtain the resources available to you.

    These financial resources and others, which you can apply for, can be found in different organizations such as the following.

- Global business accelerators (MassChallenge and others).

- Financial support for areas of innovation from foreign embassies and governments.

- Venture capitalists.

- Global business contacts for innovation exclusively.

- CDC Group development finance institution.

- University innovation business developments.

- Venture entrepreneurship.

- National Center for Entrepreneurship & Innovation.

- Entrepreneurship systems.

- Financial bankers specializing in innovation projects.

- Corporate trusts.

- Multilateral Investment Fund of the Inter-American Development Bank.

- Funds for leading-edge innovation projects.

- Foundations specializing in innovation projects.

- Subsidies for technical and professional areas, exclusively for innovation.

- Innovation mixed funds for developments in Latin America.

- Philanthropic groups.

- Technology innovations or incubators.

- Capitalist investors.

- Angel investors.

- National Institutes of Health Small Business Innovation Research.

- Innovation investors in the private sector, with subsidies from European countries in partnership with companies from Latin America or the United States.

- Start-ups.

- TuApp.org.

- Young Business Talents.

Financial resources is another term for capital support that will allow you to start your innovation or activity for your project. These resources constitute the foundation of your process, for which you will look into different organizations and search for all types of funds or financial assistance that is available to you. To obtain this support, you will be required to fulfill all the specifications stipulated by the agency or organization in exchange for the opportunity to compete and receive the funds, which will be awarded to the best idea as described in the final document.

2. **Educational Resources**
   These resources are all the options that give you access to learning and training opportunities, whether new or continuing, in a technical, professional, or research area that relates to the innovation of your product, service, or result, and that you need to acquire or improve to gain the necessary experience to engage in your innovation. These educational resources are divided as follows.

   a. Financial Education

   b. Bibliographical Resources

   c. Educational Material

These resources are available through private or public agencies that provide educational opportunities to learn about an area of your interest that will help you develop your innovation project. These organizations might make nonrefundable financial aid available to provide you with the knowledge and training needed to help you expand your idea in technical areas or research, or in any other type of training needed to expand the project and support the experimental development of your methodology.

There are organizations that administer and provide this type of resource, that support and offer innovation programs to the public. You will have to present an introduction document of no more than three pages, as described in Chapter 2, where you will briefly lay out your idea and its basic features, as a way to share your project, simply and concisely. Generally, the organizations that provide this type of assistance, which you should fully take advantage of, are universities, foundations that promote innovation programs, charitable organizations, research institutes, and foreign organizations, among others.

b. Bibliographical Resources
These resources include any reference material that you can use or consult. You might be able to search online for publications or historical data in public or private libraries. I recommend that you register with the various library systems before using or reproducing any material obtained from internet searches through these sources.

c. Educational material
These materials include any resources provided by centers or organizations that put at your disposal any work-related equipment or material that supports the development of your innovation project.

Some educational centers or organizations allow the use of computers, internet services, telephone, fax, printers, workstations, or cubicles, among others, which will help you develop or write your innovation project. These centers or organizations usually include universities, business centers, chambers of commerce, employment offices, and innovation centers, among others.

3. **Human Resources**
These resources include any formula, instruction, training, talent, experience, planning, knowledge, ideas, projections, plans, consultation, or advising related to specialized personnel, both technical and professional, capable of training, guiding, or contributing their knowledge in any of their areas of expertise or knowledge of any person participating in an innovation project as it relates to the collaboration in the development of its plan. These support human resources can be found in universities and technology centers, private industry, employment service centers, research institutions, and incubators, among others.

4. **Material Resources**
These resources are the aggregate of infrastructure and operational tools that play a part in the development of an innovation project. You can find these resources in universities, employment agencies, chambers of commerce, businesses, libraries, idea incubators, business centers of various industry branches, and other places. These organizations might provide private work stations or cubicles, and computer and office equipment needed for you to develop and write your introduction document and the final document.

The time factor in the management of a project refers mainly to the periods or duration, phases or selected stages that allow an idea to materialize. The transformation process of the activities that you need to implement to develop an innovation is included in planning a project. The purpose of the planning time is to allow doing more in less time. The purpose of the time function, as it relates to the management of a project, is to develop and implement the planning of every activity involved in taking your innovative idea to fruition within a given time frame. The aspect of time in a technical-scientific document is laid out precisely and deliberately, while in a document related to a professional field, this is done continuously and incrementally during its planning process.

In the management of a project, time represents the period that you allot for a specific function or job that you plan to carry out to develop the innovation and then be able to schedule it and know its deadlines, phases, resources, dates, duration of the activity, intervals, elements, opportunities, guides, periods, strategic progress, and proposals, to name a few.

An important time factor in the development of an innovation project is coordination, which entails knowing how to link your knowledge of all the activities that you plan to execute. You will implement this process in the realization of your activities as it relates to the time required to fulfill or complete all those activities, coordinating the execution of the functions with the time needed.

You will generate a plan to create a budget or expenditure sheet of all the human and material resources needed to carry out the activities of your innovation project. Developing a budget is essential, because you learn to maximize the value of your product, service, or result. In this way you will be able to have an overview of the total cost for the production of your innovation and to determine how you could maximize the value of your product or service. Chapters 3 and 4 will help you develop a budget, which is important to complete to be aware of the individual costs for the different areas involved in your innovation project, while also being aware of the total cost for the innovation of your product, service, or result.

SECTION 7
CONTROL

The control and monitoring process is a system for verifying the coordination and progress of all the activities that take place during the execution of an innovation project. It will help you maintain awareness of the components and their interactions at any given time in the control and monitoring of a project aimed at producing transformative changes in the pursuit of innovation.

Also, the application of each component will make the direction of the project clear as you move closer to your goal and will act as a gauging mechanism to certify all the activities and actions as you move toward the culmination of your product, service, or result.

CHAPTER 7

CONTROLLING AND MONITORING A PROJECT

Controlling and monitoring an innovation project should be a continuous and efficient process, especially if the plan includes experimental aspects to create a new product, service, or result. This step is extremely important, because it helps you oversee and analyze the entire process at all times to establish whether the objectives are being met, to control budgetary issues, to ensure that the process is working properly, and to confirm that the activities described in your plan are performing as planned. In addition, it tracks the progress of the scope and limits of the main activity.

The control and monitoring of the actions that you perform in the process of carrying out an innovation is effective once you develop a plan for every task or function described. This close observation is applied to every component or element that contributes to the transformative innovation, which helps achieve a single goal within that process. This is where you begin to record and monitor the process that you laid out. It is a record, because it is important for you to understand the mechanics of the activities or the tasks that contribute to the production and development of the innovation results.

A guideline is established to give you the ability to delegate or shift the direction of the specific responsibilities of each collaborator and of the different skills they contribute. In addition, it can fulfill a single function, which is monitoring the progress of a plan to achieve the product's full potential in terms of deadlines and budget effectiveness.

The development of the control and monitoring process follows the actions that lead to the final objective. It is designed, considering the parameters and scope of the project, to aid in completing the innovation process and achieve the desired results. Developing a control and monitoring process will help you expand your ability to make any needed changes in the execution of the plan.

You should follow an orderly plan to ensure the best outcome of all the functions needed to carry out any activity that you include or exclude in the development of the process, especially in your methodology. This will reveal important elements or components that contribute to the completion of any phase that might have a problem or that requires control, and thus will allow you to monitor how relevant they are to the fulfillment of the main objective. Later, I will describe the importance of these components.

The purpose of the control and monitoring process is to verify and observe the continuity of the progress to ensure that the planned objective is being met, to provide its estimated value, and to assess its duration. You will be able to monitor the procedures, make changes during the innovation process, in the order in which that verification process has been laid out.

This way you will be able to guarantee the orderly execution of the steps established for any changes that you make during the experimental phase, the design of your work and operation method, in other words, considering all the required activities. It will also help you make necessary changes and assessments during the continuous control and monitoring process to ensure the success of the desired objective.

What Are The Components and How Do They Work?

The elements of a control and monitoring process include the external factors that support the overall process, such as the production, perspective, revision, effectiveness, implementation, success, and productivity of the product, service, or result that you are pursuing in the process of the innovation transformation. Also, these external factors will trigger the processes of the different channels to help implement innovation. Embedded in this process are certain verification, monitoring, and development features that help you establish priorities as a way to overcome any potential limitations present in your methodology or experimental design.

The components govern the functions and the characteristics that mark the beginning of a record. Also, they reflect the progress made in the completion of the activities during the process of transformation of your product, service, or result. This process should be applied to any change, adjustment, authorization, observation, communication, approval, and verification, because whenever you make any changes to the control and monitoring of your innovation process, it could affect the completion of your objectives.

These components are essential at the verification and observation stage of your innovation process to promote maximum impact and to produce results when you are creating a work methodology. Dealing with components at this stage requires the adjustment of each function that you process and think about for you to maintain complete control during the execution phase. Figure 7.1 shows the most common components of the development of a control and monitoring process, which is carried out in steps. You will be able to decide when these steps are activated during the process.

You can use project planning to guide you and to control the multiple activities and secondary activities that take part in the innovation transfer of your product, both in the timing and the duration during the transformation process.

Figure 7.1

Control and Monitoring Process

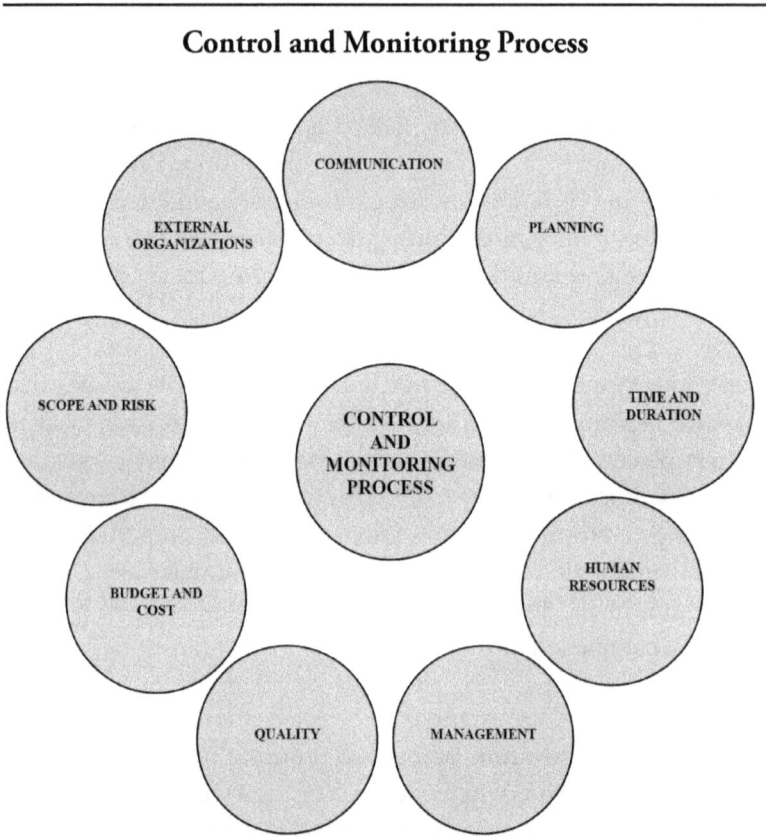

Interaction of the Components during the Control and Monitoring Process

---

It is important to make use of the components when implementing the process of controlling and monitoring the project during the innovation process, where the components are automatically subjected to cross interactions that lead in different directions within the framework of the project. Applying control and monitoring processes consists of carrying out the original plan or method, which creates a record of, and a direction for, the design of the existing work methodology, whose goal is to render an innovative result. Besides, it will gradually help you achieve the fullest potential when approaching a final product. Next, I will describe the roles played by the most common elements of a control and monitoring process.

1. **Communication**

This fundamental and essential aspect of a control and monitoring process must be part of the management of every project and its individual areas of development. It is not possible to make progress without communication. In the course of this innovation process, communication between the principal investigator and the team of collaborators in the different areas of the process must be constant. This relationship refers to the connection established between you, the principal investigator, and all the parts, team, materials, and components of the experimental design involved, in the achievement of your product, service, or result. In reality, communication, together with all the elements that take part in a control and monitoring process, is the key component for the successful development and conclusion of a project. Communication has a direct link to the development of every objective that you intend to obtain from a result.

You should be able to set up remote electronic communication channels for the continuous monitoring throughout the innovation process for the analysis of data, to maintain contact with personnel through memos, or through internal communication devices, such as smartboards, which will give electronic access to the project plan and progress to every researcher, among others. In the course of these communications, you will be able to remind everyone about the end goal, deadlines, problems-solutions, results, milestones, and parameters, using a prepared plan, where you will lay out the channels for the continuous, scheduled, and efficient communication during the evolution of your product, service, or result that you intend to generate.

2. Planning

This element is your ally and constant companion during every control and monitoring process that you work on, because it is the guideline and blueprint for all your actions. It is the orderly, organized, documented, and verified work methodology that you develop and put in place. During the planning process, you consult the plan that you have created to check the progress of the transformative results in the process of the innovation of a product, service, or result that you are pursuing.

Also, you will be able to verify the limitations, progress, time, scope, and every aspect of the functions described that you could think of for the planning of the confirmation process for the control and monitoring of a project. This way you will turn all the information into an organized blueprint for the completion of a job. There will be times when the design has areas that need to be modified or changed, and you will keep a record of all those changes that are needed to access and make progress in your methodology so you can be more productive in achieving the desired results.

Excellent organizational skills are essential during the control and monitoring phase of a plan's development, as well as establishing control mechanisms to record any changes that you might make. In addition, during this phase, you will have opportunities to observe the sequence of your design's activities to give you a glimpse of the direction of your product, service, or result and look ahead at the final result that you are hoping to achieve.

3. Time and Duration

This stage of the planning process is where you establish the timing and duration of the activities in cycles or stages in a linear manner, which trigger the duration of each activity until the required objective is completed. The control and monitoring of the evolution will be completed in stages.

The activities should be carried out in multiple controlled and monitored stages to ensure their completion. Time refers to the completion of an activity or function, and it is important to efficiently allocate time for the various activities. For the control and monitoring process, time and duration are predetermined during the development of the innovation to be able to illustrate each required action with a limited continuous line. By doing this, the activities will be able to operate independently based on their functions and times. This is why good schedule planning is important and effective.

4. **Human Resources**
    This essential component of the control and monitoring phase is where you manage all the participants of a project and develop a work methodology to innovate a product, service, or result that you are pursuing. Human resources are fundamental for the development of a work methodology or design aimed at implementing a specific type of knowledge and transforming it into results to create a new product or service. During the transformation process, you will also be developing a plan.

Human resources are a direct connection between the management of a project and the success or failure of your intended objective. The aggregate of all the participants represents the piece that completes the circle that provides productive strength, which generates a transformative path to change. When you combine intelligent management with human resources equipped with specific tools, you are injecting creativity, wisdom, and guided decision-making power, and broadcasting what you wish to accomplish to all the participants. In addition, you are encouraging the sharing of new ideas that might contribute to better results.

The control and monitoring process applied to all human resources is an essential element of project development. You should always encourage a collaborative atmosphere for all participants when performing the activities, which could include examining qualitative options of the elements in progress, challenges, components, operations, and errors, among others. This way you will be able to carry out your objectives collaboratively.

The option to implement an action, or to use it to facilitate the completion of a task, entails the engagement of others to fulfill the desired result. Besides, by doing this, you deploy an operational capability to modify any procedural changes in the development of an experimental design, which might have qualitative potential to speed up, maintain, or reproduce actions in the development of innovative strategies.

5. **Management**

This component oversees the application of the control and monitoring process for the management of the strategies, resources, timing of the activities, and budgets that form part of the work methodology designed specifically to achieve the desired innovation outcomes of a product, service, or result. You must establish a control for the effectiveness and growth of the strategy you use.

If it is not suitable or it is slow, it will trigger a change control that will replace that element with one that is better or more flexible. This will allow you to monitor the overall functioning of the strategy, to observe the performance and progress of the resources, and to evaluate the time and operating budget in your work methodology. I mention the term *work action,* which means setting forth a plan or original outline, executing your decisions, carrying out technical activities, applying executive functions, and performing control and monitoring negotiations.

Good management requires monitoring the four functional elements according to your plan, to encourage the growth of your innovation. The engagement of resources includes knowing how to control and take advantage of the options that present themselves during the development of a methodology. The management component ensures the participation of all the areas of the methodology that enables you to carry the innovation to fruition on time, with an accurate estimation of when it will be completed, a well-defined budget, and a record of accomplished and completed tasks.

6. **Quality**
    This component of the control and monitoring process refers to the distinctive characteristics of your transformational methodology or the final product, service, or result that you plan to innovate. Therefore, you will use qualities that identify specific regular and individual features described in the methodology or established in the experimental design that you intend to follow. In addition, it governs the qualitative certification of the execution of the results.

    During the application of the monitoring process, you must keep in mind the details of your unique innovation, which will be driven by the elements laid out in your work methodology. You should establish your own specifications that stand out during the process to help you monitor and complete them. There are different technical and professional areas where a quality component can be carried out together with the actions performed during the creative development of a product or service and thus be able to understand the critical point for the innovation's optimum reach.

7. Budget and Cost

These elements form an integral part of the control and monitoring process, which verify, maintain, and guide the direct and indirect expenses allotted for each one of the elements of the budget to control the funds available for the development of your innovation product, service, or result. It is the only component of the control and monitoring phase that is applied before the work methodology begins, at the time your company receives the funds from an organization to carry out your innovation project.

When you plan a budget, it is a good idea to request two or three quotes for each item, material, or equipment that you plan to purchase. This way you will be able to select the best quality material for your job at the best price. The effect of a budget on the control and monitoring of an innovation project is determined by the expenses incurred to carry out each planned activity to achieve the following.

- Objectives of a project.
- Competent and satisfactory results.
- Completion of the project as scheduled, well managed, and with an exact and carefully estimated budget.

8. Scope and Risk

This control and monitoring element relates to the attention required in an innovation project. The term *contingency* refers to unforeseen events that you might encounter in any phase or stage of your experimental design process such as critical points, risks, and maximum limitations or scope, which you should always keep in mind and describe in a section of your project.

In this step, the control and monitoring process will raise an alert or demand your full attention at the critical or beneficial moment that might require greater attention and oversight during the development of that phase of the process. It will also reflect the scope or limits of your experiment's work methodology.

9. **External Organizations**
These are essential partners in the control and monitoring process of an innovation project. External organizations are those that provide and make available financial resources to carry out innovation projects in various areas. The first step of this phase is your introduction document, where you will express your interest in turning your idea into an innovation project. The second step is the delivery of your complete project or final document, whose purpose is to bid for financial assistance, which is how you initiate your entrepreneurial project.

These external organizations establish a series of requirements that you will have to abide by, which might require monthly, quarterly, or final progress reports to maintain a reliable and updated budget record throughout the project. Even if the organization does not require these documents, it is recommended to voluntarily present a report of your activities every ninety days and an expense sheet every three months.

The control and monitoring process requires close communication between you and the external organization, both in terms of the operation's activities and the expenses incurred during the execution of your project. Also, if you can secure additional support and financial resources for your innovation from other external organizations, it is a good idea to let the original organization know.

The control and monitoring process as a whole will provide an overview of the direction and scale of the scope of the project that you intend to develop, complete with activities and a path to devising and gauging the product, service, or result that you wish to achieve. This process creates an opportunity for checking and outlining the activities required for the qualitative arrangement of the changes that are needed for completing your innovation.

END OF THE CIRCLE OF INNOVATION

After reviewing all the components of the circle of innovation in previous chapters, this last chapter relates to the completion or conclusion of an innovation project. This component signals the end of operations of the work methodology and its final result. It refines the main areas of the administrative goal, and it lays out the future paths for your product, service, or result after the objectives have been accomplished.

CHAPTER 8

FINALIZING THE INNOVATION PROJECT

You can now combine the tools that have been presented in each of the areas of the circle of innovation. In this book, you have learned how to lay out each one of them. Starting with the visualization of the potential of an idea for unveiling a concept that you can develop and turn into an innovative product, service, or result that you would like to pursue. Then you will be able to process each one of these components successfully to reach this last phase and, in doing so, conclude your project to be able to lay it out in its totality in a final document.

In this chapter, you will develop a basic checklist that finalizes or concludes an innovation project, and caps the circle of innovation, as represented in Figure 8.1. This figure includes the various components that interact with one another in each of the stages, with the different perspectives of the project's main actions carried through to the final revisions. If you carefully look at the entire innovation method, you should be able to see all the components turning clockwise, with the main components fluctuating with individual interactions, following an orderly process until the innovation method is complete.

There is a space in the middle where you can note every item and component and describe how each element plays a part in the process that stems from each component. You will be able to brainstorm based on the information that stems from them to transform or modify the desired results by leveraging their best characteristics. You will also be able to generate additional distinct variants to help you achieve your innovation, either for technical-scientific projects or for a professional field.

You started with an idea for an innovation project, you laid out results and presented them to create a product or service, which you then carried out according to your plan and experimental design. This idea revolves around various components, assembled and incorporated in an active, coordinated manner, that reveal their potential as you progress, always aiming at surpassing the maximum result that you have in mind for your innovation, where the final step consists of the discovery of elements that you will have to evaluate during the process.

Figure 8.1

End of a Project, Last Phase of the Elements That Form a Circle of Innovation

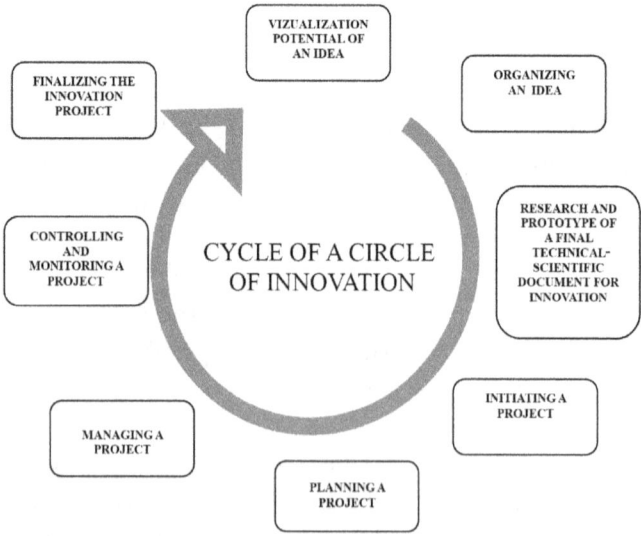

The conclusion of a project with all its innovative components marks the end of the processing and innovation phase of the idea. You should submit to verification the characteristics of this process and the most important sections of the project's plan, which includes these three areas.

1. End of operations of an experimental design or work methodology.

2. Conclusion of a project's administrative or management phase.

3. Final elements that follow the completion of an innovation project.

1. End of Operations
The end of the experimental design or work methodology is characterized by the conclusion and thorough verification of the main blueprint and its functions, which once completed will result in the product or service with its specific characteristics, according to the innovative elements of your field. Also, it is at that moment that the objectives, procedures, and planning of the idea that you formulated can be considered tested and completed. You will have produced your final entrepreneurial result.

In finalizing this stage of the process, you will have verified that every procedure included in the work methodology has been completed and that it has produced results, including parameters, limits, and other variants that form part of your experimental design. You will verify your data to show that you have achieved the projected results.

With the completion of the operational and functional phase, you achieve the first step on your way to the final test, which is making sure that completing all the experimental stages or phases of an innovation leads to the success of the project. This way you will generate the final blueprint for a design and through its implementation create a product, service, or result that will have the basic elements of a product ready for market and application.

The end of operations of a project's experimental phase marks the direct correlation between the culmination of a project and the conclusion of the management phase, because data from both areas come into play and converge and contribute to the completion of the project.

2. Conclusion

The conclusion of the administrative phase is where you lay out the terms for the management, direction, and administrative directives for the project, including the delivery of a final document to organizations that provide funds for innovation projects. Therefore, this final step should include the following basic concepts.

- Completed objectives with the appropriate innovative results.

- Updated, detailed, and accurate budget.

- Timely delivery of the final document.

These basic concepts are represented in Figure 8.2, as the three main areas of the administrative phase, which consists of the management of the project during the innovation development process. Each area presents elements of related activities with various conclusions or terms that you plan to pursue. Some of the practices are listed that you will carry out in each of the areas.

Figure 8.2

Essential Elements in the Management of a Project

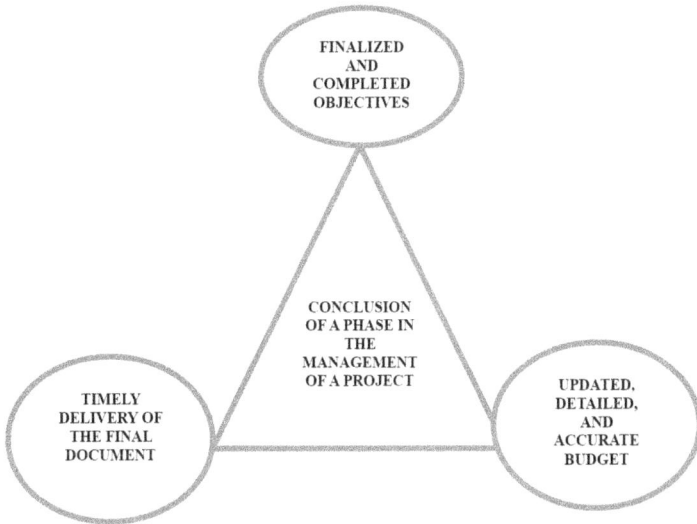

The area of completed objectives includes the operational results of a transformation carried out with a goal in mind; here you will complete the experimental phase of an innovation. This is the segment where you manage and negotiate the end of a series of data with results and conclusions. It will be reflected on the products, services, or results that you obtain from following a methodology.

It is important to use a plan and to have strict checkpoints or mechanisms for the compliance of every objective from the plan that you are following, which is the essence of this chapter. This area includes the delivery of an activity report in draft or final format, according to the requirements stipulated by the specific organization. You should include certain annotations in your plan, such as the delivery date for the report, means represented, and amount of time requested.

Generally, the organizations that require these types of clauses, such as delivery of an activity report, functions, or results, grant 90 to 120 days after initiating the innovation. Other organizations require one single report at the end of each objective or upon completion of the project.

You should include in this section all the documentation related to agreements, contracts, commitment letters, leased material, human resources, use and final delivery of laboratories, among others, which will contribute to savings in your budget. In addition, included in this section will be the permits or remodels that you might have to carry out during that period. Also, the conclusion of the management phase will include the writing and delivery of letters of appreciation to organizations that collaborate directly or indirectly with the project or that provide any consulting services during your innovation.

The section of the updated, detailed and accurate budget is where you show compliance with the planned budget to carry out your project. For this you will write a detailed report of the updated expenses from the funds that you received from the granting organization. Within the budget, you will describe the five most important sections of your expenses (see the budget descriptions in Chapters 3 and 4) that you will incur during the development of your project. These budget figures should be accurate and up to date.

The timely delivery of a final document is where you include the complete list of activities carried out and completed in your project, that is, the execution of all the aspects of your innovation process, whether they are related to management or to the constructive functions required to produce results. All of this should be laid out and delivered by the date established by the organization that grants funds for innovation projects.

3. Final Elements

The elements that follow the completion of an innovation project include all the external aspects of the project that come afterward, in other words, anything that ensures the continuity of the subsequent steps and what comes after. Once the final document for your innovation project has been completed and delivered, you will define the avenues, studies, and projections of the opportunities to move forward beyond the final document, granted you have been successful at securing funds to continue with the following steps.

A. Market study.

B. Market launch.

C. Establishing a business.

A. Market Study

A market study begins with an analysis or study of the market for the product, service, or result that you have generated from your innovation process. You will determine the basis and state of the market and purchasing results that you obtain at the local, regional, national, and international levels. In addition, you should include logistics, preferential marketing, sales, prices, and availability, among others.

The organization where you apply for funds will give you guidelines for the marketing phase. It is a good idea to continue researching information about the market study for the product, service, or result that you pursue, before you proceed with the second phase with the fund-granting organization. That will save you time and give you more opportunities to collect development data and be able to carry out this phase to fruition.

B. Market Launch

You begin the marketing process by analyzing information data on the eve of establishing an entrepreneurial business, and it consists of a summary of research-based data, which will produce, among others, marketing tactics, types of markets, demographics, and types of consumers for your entrepreneurial venture. This information is processed or analyzed by looking at the figures, which will indicate the viability of your innovative business.

You should be able to find this information on the internet in the statistics or information technology section or in the census for the particular country where you intend to market your product. You should analyze and evaluate the most important data, with a wide vision of the market sector that could benefit from your results and contribute to the value, negotiation, and marketing of your product, service, or result.

Also, the research process will help you unveil information about precedents for commercial models, which will manifest the level of confidence needed to be able to confront a healthy competition from innovative products or outcomes that are similar to yours.

C. Establishing a Business

The opening of an establishment or business where you can exhibit or place a final product, service, or result that you have innovated will be the pinnacle of your innovation project. Opening the doors of a business means putting your innovation product on a pedestal where everybody will be able to admire it, whether it is a brick-and-mortar venue, the internet, a catalog, exhibit stand, or in any other medium; this is the ultimate goal of the design and development that you carried out.

All of this is the result of the plan that you devised to take you to the final stage. The opening of a business in an area of innovation implies bringing your authentic idea to fruition, transformed by your knowledge and development following a creative and entrepreneurial path. And it is on this new path that you move forward with skill and confidence, a great deal of ingenuity, and a desire to innovate, combining a number of elements such as knowledge, resolve, creativity, and initiative.

Complete success!

"IF HUMANS CAN WALK IN SPACE IN A STATE OF WEIGHTLESSNESS, IMAGINE WHAT YOU CAN CREATE OR DEVELOP."

CARLOS S. MONSIVAIS

www.ingramcontent.com/pod-product-compliance
Lightning Source LLC
Chambersburg PA
CBHW031852200326
41597CB00012B/377